ALL UNDER HEAVEN

p. 27, n. 31, review article on 'popular religion'.
p. 29, n. 39, S. Endicott source?
☆ p. 34, n. 51, key source on spirit possession & Xty in Taiwan.

p. 59, identifies 3 groups, esp. "old" & "new" TSPMers.

☆ p. 60, n. 7, useful source on Korean religion / Xty
p. 62. Liu Xiaofeng & CCR

ch. 7, the survey of PRC students in UK, worth pondering - some good quotes, e.g. bottom of p. 105.

Vp

This publication is no. 17 in the series KTC (KERK EN THEOLOGIE IN CONTEXT - CHURCH AND THEOLOGY IN CONTEXT) of the Faculty of Theology of the Catholic University of Nijmegen, The Netherlands.

Chinese Tradition and Christian Life
in the People's Republic of China

ALL UNDER HEAVEN

edited by
Alan Hunter and Don Rimmington

UITGEVERSMAATSCHAPPIJ J.H. KOK – KAMPEN 1992

Acknowledgements

The editors would like to express particular gratitude to Maggie Whyte for her enormous help with the editorial work. At one stage her efforts kept the project going. Greg Benton, Peter Nix and Yo Tomita also provided much-needed assistance with recalcitrant computer disks.

We are grateful to Professor Arnulf Camps and Drs. Kristin De Troyer for their enthusiastic participation in the publication of this volume, and to the staff at Kok Pharos for organizing production so efficiently.

This collection of papers and the conference at which they were first presented received generous support from the University of Leeds, England.

CIP-GEGEVENS KONINKLIJKE BIBLIOTHEEK, DEN HAAG

Hunter, Alan

All under heaven: Chinese tradition and Christian life in the People's Republic of China/ Alan Hunter and Don Rimmington. - Kampen: Kok. - (Kerk en theologie in context, ISSN 0922-9086; dl. 17)
Met bibliogr.
ISBN 90-242-7381-1
NUGI 631
Trefw.: kerk en maatschappij; China.

Alan Hunter and Don Rimmington (eds)

Licensed edition, published by Uitgeversmaatschappij J.H. Kok b.v., P.O. Box 130, 8260 AC Kampen, The Netherlands
Cover design: Dik Hendriks
Zetwerk: Elgraphic bv, Schiedam
ISBN 90 242 7381 1/NUGI 631

CONTENTS

CONTENTS

INTRODUCTION

Alan Hunter and Don Rimmington

What was known as "the communist world" has undergone profound changes in the past few years: the student demonstrations in the spring of 1989 in Beijing, the subsequent attack on unarmed civilians by the People's Liberation Army, the sudden collapse of regimes throughout East Europe and the crisis in the former Soviet Union. The Christian world, meanwhile, has been undergoing changes which are equally profound if less dramatic: churches are losing influence in many industrialized countries but Christianity is experiencing vigorous growth in Africa and Asia. China is in a unique position: its communist government and social system has survived at least this round of protest, but, contrary to expectations, Christianity is beginning to emerge as a force in Chinese society.

Western scholarship on China since 1949 has tended to focus on a limited range of themes. Before 1980, dozens of volumes attempted to analyze the inner workings of the Chinese Communist Party (CCP) and there were major efforts to understand economic, military and diplomatic issues. In the 1980s western researchers were allowed greater access to Chinese society, which resulted in a number of sociological studies on topics such as family, gender, work and education. Communism was perceived as less of a threat to the west: the new economic policies adopted in Beijing persuaded most observers that China was a respectable member of the world community, and moreover had huge potential as consumer of industrial products and provider of cheap labour.

Before 1989, it seems to have been taken for granted that the CCP was of supreme importance in Chinese society, that its power was unquestionable and that it would rule China for many decades to come. By 1991 few people subscribed to this view. Even in Beijing, the seat of government, everybody was wondering when and how the CCP would collapse. Chinese intellectuals regarded the top leadership as isolated, lower administrators as disillusioned, the urban population as disgusted by corruption and the slow rate of economic progress.

Now may be a suitable time to reconsider issues which have been largely neglected in the study of modern China. One such area is undoubtedly religion. To the surprise of many observers, both Chinese and westerners, the 1980s saw a revival of religious activity in China. From 1949 until 1979 the practice of religion had been repressed and believers had suffered various forms of administrative sanctions. After 1979, apart from local difficulties, the Chinese people were able to conduct authorized religious activities and also took advantage of the relatively liberal atmosphere to engage in all kinds of unauthorized ones. Protestant Christianity in particular grew very fast in the early 1980s, reportedly causing considerable concern to the CCP leadership. Their anxieties intensified after the political changes in East Europe, in which Christian churches were deeply involved.

It seems, then, that the study of religion in China deserves more attention. The revival of the 1980s showed that religions had greater endurance and deeper roots in Chinese culture than observers had anticipated, and events of 1989 and 1990 showed that they could have political implications too. The most dynamic religion in the 1980s was Protestantism, but this cannot be considered in isolation from other issues: the evolving traditions of popular culture, the Catholic church, the spiritual and moral condition of Chinese youth and so on. Scholars working in these areas attended a conference on "Chinese Tradition and Christian Life in the People's Republic of China" held at the University of Leeds from 29 to 31 March 1990. The papers in this volume were presented at the conference, which was jointly organized by the University's Department of East Asian Studies and Department of Theology and Religious Studies.

This conference took a consciously inter-disciplinary approach, bringing together British, Chinese and European scholars with backgrounds in sinology, church history, social science and religious studies. The central concern was to investigate from different perspectives the changing role of Christianity in China in the 1980s and to review the profound impact of the decade's political, social and economic transformation on spiritual values and Christian practice. There was particular interest in the growth of church membership and patterns of conversion. The degree and nature of state control over religion was another major theme: the extent of new restrictions after June 1989 and the churches' responses will be of vital importance in the next few years.

Hunter and Rimmington (Religion and Social Change in Contemporary China) give an overview of the context for the Christian revival. They review the range of available sources of information, the changes in Chinese society under the impact of industrialization, the crisis in political religion, the place of religion in an atheist state and the emergence of new strands of popular religion.

Dr Chan Kim-Kwong (A Chinese Perspective on the Interpretation of the Chinese Government's Religious Policy) considers the administration of religious affairs in traditional China and points out continuities in the policies and methods adopted by the current regime. The theme of government control is also central to the paper by Feuchtwang (The Old and the New: A Commentary on the Control of Popular Religion in the PRC), but is approached from a different angle. Feuchtwang explores the ways in which the government, through its cultural bureaux, exploits or rejects various features of popular traditions and religion in the attempt to create a modern, national, Chinese political culture.

Whyte and Tang are both experienced researchers and writers from church research institutes, and thus in an excellent position to review the experiences of the Protestant and Catholic churches in recent years. Whyte (Some Reflections on Protestant Life in China) addresses a wide range of issues. He traces Christianity's past confrontations with Confucian and Communist ideologies to its present encounter with the uncertainties of contemporary society. He poses the need for the Protestant church to evolve a critical theology to sustain its identity, to maintain unity against a background of increasing fragmentation and diversity. Tang (A Year of Confrontation: The Catholic Church in China in 1989) throws light on the complex relationships of the official and unofficial Catholic churches and their attitudes to the Vatican. He also presents evidence of the pressures that have come to bear on the Catholic community since the June 4 events.

Feng and Benton (Chinese Youth Today: The Crisis of Belief) provide a vigorous analysis of the differing attitudes and aspirations of a sequence of generations in China. The cynicism and nihilism current among Chinese youth may appear indifferent to morality and belief, but they may also be instrumental in generating a new climate of opinion which rejects a persistently Stalinist system of government. Hunter and Rimmingtons's empirical survey of religion among Chinese students (Train up a Child: Attitudes towards Religion and Atheism among Chinese Students) finds that about 20% of young, educated Chinese appear to have an interest in spiritual or religious matters, 20% take a clear anti-religious stance, and the remaining 60% show some interest in, or at least are not opposed to, religious ideas. The survey also reveals considerable interest in existential questions.

Yu and Hood offer two different perspectives. Yu (The Relevance of Christian Humanism to the Quest for Democracy in China) writes from Hong Kong. He points up both contrasts and links between the Chinese and Christian humanist traditions. He speculates whether some fusion of these traditions may be the key to the development of democracy in China: a question which is close to the heart of many Christian intellectuals in China itself. Hood was himself a missionary in China shortly before 1949. His paper (What Has Changed? A Vignette of Shantou) describes his return to Shantou after an absence of almost forty years. He found that his former Presbyterian church was still very much alive and that it seemed to have established a more secure place within the local community.

In his paper (The Christian-Chinese Encounter), Hastings sums up some of the themes of the conference and places them in the perspective of global changes. This century has seen gains and losses for Chinese Christians, but Professor Hastings ponders whether their latest harsh encounter with Marxist authorities may paradoxically pave the way for the founding of a Christian presence within the mainstream of Chinese tradition. Finally, literature affords interesting insights into the Chinese appreciation of religious values. Francesca Rhys (When Dusk Disappeared: Religion in a Contemporary Short Story) presents some extracts in translation, together with her reflections on this unusual appearance of religion in modern Chinese fiction.

We hope this book is of interest to readers from different backgrounds; it does not demand specialist knowledge of sinology or religious studies, although the authors make contributions to these disciplines. We have employed the *hanyu pinyin* system of romanization, although a very few names and words, such as 'Tao' and its cognates, have been left in their more familiar form. A short booklist is appended.

The editors would like to thank the sponsors whose generous donations made the conference possible: the University of Leeds, the Society for the Promotion of Christian Knowledge, the Sino-British Fellowship Trust, the Great Britain-China Centre and the British Council of Churches. We are also grateful to the Leverhulme Trust for funding the three year research project "Christianity in China Today" out of which this conference arose.

1. RELIGION AND SOCIAL CHANGE IN CONTEMPORARY CHINA

Alan Hunter and Don Rimmington

Signs of religious revival have struck many visitors to China in recent years. Churches and temples are being built or renovated. Popular religious activities are in evidence, seminaries are training a new generation of pastors, services in big cities are well attended. Christianity has experienced considerable growth, Buddhism and folk traditions are better supported than at any time since the 1940s. Non-Han peoples retain a deep commitment to Islam and Lamaist Buddhism. Yet all this is taking place in a country which is industrializing, where secular education is improving and scientific knowledge becoming more widespread than ever in the past[1]. Moreover state policy aims to discourage religion and religious groups are sometimes subject to administrative sanctions. The state education system is resolutely atheist, faith is often represented as reactionary superstition in the press and evangelism is illegal.

This paper aims to offer an overview of the current state of religion in this environment which at first sight is so hostile. It is necessarily of a preliminary and exploratory nature. First there is a dearth of empirical data. Foreigners wishing to conduct fieldwork in China can face various difficulties, and research into religion has not been accorded a high priority by the Chinese academic establishment, which is primarily concerned with the modernization programme[2].

A major weakness is that information about Buddhism is even less accessible than that concerning Christianity which has been studied in some depth by church research centres. This represents a serious gap in our understanding since Buddhism probably has a far greater following than other religions. Practically the only sources available at present are issues of the official Buddhist Association journal *Fayin* and occasional reports in the Chinese press, usually lamenting the large numbers of people currently engaged in pilgrimages

1. Official sources also recognise the rapid expansion of religious activities, viewing them as a source of concern. See for example the major policy document 'Religion and Feudal Superstition', *Renmin Ribao* (People's Daily), March 15 1979; and the important official statement 'Do away with feudal superstition' translated in *FBIS* (China), K17-22, 17 January 1983. Few statistics are available concerning the number of Buddhists. Garside reports the figure of 100 million lay Buddhists quoted by a national leader in *Coming Alive: China after Mao*, London: Andre Deutsch, 1981. Religious propagation may not be carried on outside religious buildings; atheist propagation may not be carried out within them. As Philip Wickeri (*Seeking the Common Ground: Protestant Christianity, the Three Self Movement and the United Front*, Maryknoll: Orbis Books, 1989) and Holmes Welch (*Buddhism under Mao*, Cambridge, Mass.: Harvard University Press, 1972) wryly observe, the division of space is rather favourable to the latter.
2. See S. Feuchtwang, "The Study of Chinese Popular Religion in the PRC", *Revue europeene des sciences sociales*, vol 27 no 84, 1989, pp. 85-86.

and other forms of devotion. Information about Taoism is similarly scanty. We are thus in no position to offer anything like a comprehensive account of the situation.

Second, theoretical analysis of religion in China is not far developed, except in the field of social anthropology which has mostly been focused on popular religion in Taiwan. Third, we do not discuss the very important question of religion among non-Han peoples, for example Islam in Xinjiang or Buddhism in Tibet, since this is a highly specialized area which demands separate treatment. However it is essential to attempt an overview of the pattern as well as consider the details of each part.

The impact of industrialization on culture is a complex field of study, and it may be helpful to consider the issue in general terms before returning to the Chinese situation in particular. Industrialization gives rise to new physical environments, fragmentation of communities, a restructuring of the economy and people's working lives, far-reaching changes in social institutions such as the family: in short, rapid social change[3]. It can also cause a fragmentation of value-systems, whereby a single dominant ideology is threatened by a variety of institutions, commercial interests and social organizations each offering their own ideas. Individuals, often uprooted from their childhood environment, become able to adopt some and reject others, perhaps influenced by a new socio-economic context in which they are placed.

Problems in changing societies are caused not only by social and economic deprivation but by this widespread uncertainty about values or meanings. The new spirit of a society in transition is a two-edged sword. On the one hand it can allow for an openness, individuality and creativity that would be difficult to achieve in a society dominated by rigid traditions. But on the other, many individuals and communities may well lack the intellectual and emotional stability to preserve a sense of their own identity, to make reasoned choices in face of the conflicting claims of different interest groups. Accepted codes of morality lose their authority and society its cohesion.

Disruption of the old traditions was profound in Europe and the USA, but the effects were at least mitigated by the relatively gentle pace of change. In many countries this took place over two or three centuries, allowing new forms of civil society to emerge and stabilize. The process has been more sudden and the consequences often more severe where agrarian societies have been catapulted into rapid industrialization in the space of a few generations, often as a result of a modernizing élite implementing changes from above. Examples can be found in the Soviet Union under Stalin or Iran under the Shah, where violent repression was necessary to break up the old social structures, leading eventually to a resurgence of fundamentalism. We will suggest that in China, as in the Soviet Union, the modernizing élite itself espoused a sort of fundamentalism in its attempt to unify and control the population in this great enterprise.

The interplay between industrialization and religion has been particularly com-

3. See F. Milson, *Youth in a Changing Society*, London: Routledge and Kegan Paul, 1972; E. Chinoy, *Society: An Introduction to Sociology*, New York: Random House, 1967.

plex and multi-dimensional. There are powerful arguments to suggest that industrial societies are becoming more secular. But we also find a 'new' conservativism (evangelical churches in the USA), militant fundamentalism (Iran), attempts at modernization of doctrine (Roman Catholicism after Vatican II), proliferation of cults and sects (USA and West Europe), engagement in revolutionary politics (liberation theology). It appears there is no simple correlation between modernization and the disappearance of religion: events in Iran, South Africa or Poland show that religion still plays a dynamic role in the modern world, particularly in societies with acute social tensions. Perhaps instead of steadily disappearing, religious movements will continue to operate in cycles, waning at one place and time, emerging with great vigour elsewhere. The tired engineering metaphor of economics as 'base' and religion as part of 'superstructure', favoured by vulgar Marxism, seems of limited explanatory value, although unfortunately a dogmatic economic determinism is still influential in some Chinese institutions[4].

China provides a classic example of massive social change in the past century. Against a background of earlier civil wars, famines, imperialism, urbanization and overthrow of a two thousand year old imperial system, even since 1949 there have been the traumatic upheavals of land reform, political campaigns, collectivization, the Cultural Revolution, the return of family farming and rapid industrialization. A consideration or religion in the PRC should perhaps set out from the perspective of a society in the process of modernizing. One should be aware of the pitfalls of simply transferring the concept 'modernization' to China. Chinese society and its institutions are unique; sociological terms from a different context may not be appropriate. However, although still largely agrarian, China now has an industrial sector of considerable importance. The processes of social change must be taken into account.

These considerations may offer a fruitful way to reflect on questions of values and religion in China. From the experiences of other countries we might anticipate first a pervasive anomie, widespread uncertainty and psychological chaos[5]; secondly the survival of religion, not necessarily in its old forms but as a living force in society. To see to what extent these expectations are justified we will consider four areas of religious life in China. First, the values of the political élite and its 'political religion'; then the institutionalized religions which have achieved accommodation with the government; attempts to maintain or revert to folk traditions; and finally the revival of heterodox sects. These facets of religion are diverse and affect different social strata in different ways. Nevertheless they combine and influence each other in the intricate network of relationships that form Chinese society.

4. Brian Morris, *Anthropological Studies of Religion*, Cambridge University Press, 1987, provides an excellent extended commentary on more subtle and complex theories of religion from Marx, Weber and Durkheim down to contemporary theories.
5. There is a critical discussion of the concept of 'anomie' in I.M. Lewis *Ecstatic Religion*, Harmondsworth: Penguin, 1971.

Political Religion in Crisis

An important aim of any political élite is to elicit a degree of emotional support, or at least acceptance, from its people. This is often achieved through a quasi-religious use of ritual, solemn music and mythology. In the case of modern China it has commonly been observed that the CCP came to power on a tide of genuine popular enthusiasm that ebbed as time went on. As its authentic support crumbled, it made great efforts to shore up its authority, presenting the ruling élite as legitimate holders of a secure mandate. This was nothing new in China, where the state has had a religious dimension for many centuries. The imperial system was supported by an ideology that attributed divine right to the emperor, and the state power confirmed its prestige by all manner of rituals, ceremonies and sacred edicts. The formal aspect of Confucianism and emperor worship has been repudiated in China. Confucian study groups, publication programmes and rituals are promoted, but one suspects largely for the purposes of tourism and academic prestige. However the spirit of Confucianism lives on, for example in the omnipresence of hierarchical structures and the intrusive nature of the state. The new rulers after 1949 were in many respects iconoclastic, but they failed to eradicate these phenomena; rather they transformed them into the contemporary 'political religion', which is profoundly influential at many levels of Chinese society.

Marxism-Leninism, a political ideology, has been used in various countries to legitimize regimes. Among its 'religious' features, when used in this way, perhaps the most important is a sanctification of the existing social order, the creation of its own holy scriptures and saints, a sense of absolutism whereby criticism is sacrilege[6]. However, Marxism-Leninism cannot be regarded as a conventional religion because it rejects the notions of deity and transcendence, nor does it claim to give a complete answer to all existential problems, for example death – hence the qualification 'political'. The sense of 'sacredness' or 'timeless importance' is attributed not to a spiritual entity, but rather to a political system and ideology; conversely, the political élite can claim authority not only over political affairs but over the whole of social life, including traditional religious institutions[7]. Hence the derivation of Leninist policy on other religions: they are heretical alongside the revealed truth of Marxism and should be controlled or eliminated.

Political religion in this sense has been a prominent feature of Chinese life since 1949. An important element has been the almost transcendent or chiliastic perspective of the CCP, particularly under Mao: the intention to radically change the consciousness of the Chinese people, to make a revolution to touch people's souls, to move history into another era. The mechanisms by which this was attempted have been described and analyzed by many writers: re-education,

6. C. Lane, *The Rites of Rulers, Ritual in Industrial Society: The Soviet Case*, Cambridge University Press, 1981, p. 36.
7. For further discussion see also M. B. Zeldin, "The Religious Nature of Russian Marxism", in *Journal for the Scientific Study of Religion*, vol 8 no 1, 1969, pp.100-11.

political indoctrination, mass-movements and use of the media are among the most obvious. The attempt to create a quasi-religious dimension to the state demanded the replacement of traditional festivals by new national celebrations, fanatical devotion to supreme leaders endowed with quasi-divine characteristics, new forms of state ceremonial and ritual. These perhaps reached their most destructive during the Cultural Revolution, for example in the May 7th Cadre schools. Cadres, many of whom were highly educated people who had held responsible positions in society, were obliged to pray to posters of Mao, thanking him for food before meals, confessing sins and sinful thoughts, asking his blessing and requesting guidance. The overtly religious nature of Party praxis at this time is well documented in a book edited by Urban, which is indeed a strange collection of documents to emerge from a communist state[8]. This was an extreme point, but contemporary phenomena share something of the same quality, for example the rituals enacted to reaffirm loyalty to the Party leadership in the summer of 1989.

On the question of ritual and ceremonial there are interesting comparisons to be made with the Soviet Union, where the leadership consciously elaborated a system of new social rituals to replace old religious ones. They promoted the use of symbols such as the Hammer and Sickle, the Red Banner, the Blazing Torch; light, height and fire; colour; verbal and musical expressions; hero creation; militarized body movements. Lane interprets Soviet ritual as one of the most important strategies utilized to maintain social control: "an instrument of cultural management enabling political élites... to gain acceptance for a general system of norms and values congruent with their interpretation of Marxism-Leninism[9]". Such 'cultural management' was necessary because the gap between official rhetoric and social reality was so great: Marxism became a conservative rationalization for the preservation of the status quo.

Important as is state ritual in China, perhaps an even better illustration of the CCP's quasi-religious stance is its mode of discourse, which bears striking similarities to that of theocratic organizations. One can find much food for thought in the interesting paper 'What is Islamic Fundamentalism?' by Professor Nader Saiedi[10]. One can note surprising parallels with CCP ideology at certain stages of its development. Some 'characteristics and forms of Islamic fundamentalism' discussed in Saiedi's paper are: repressive interpretation of orthodoxy; legitimized suppression, discrimination, brutality and violation of human rights; unity of church and state; explicit deprivation of the non-believer from various social and political rights; predominance of evil symbols; characterization of everything western and modern in terms of sin and evil; mythology of martyrdom and bloody struggle; scriptural literalism and rejection of critical rationality; obsession with purity, sexual repression, elimination of minority cul-

8. G. R. Urban (ed.), *The Miracles of Chairman Mao: a Compendium of Devotional Literature 1966-1970*, London: Stacey, 1971.
9. Lane, op. cit., p. 25.
10. N. Saiedi, "What is Islamic Fundamentalism?" in J. K. Hadden and A. Shupe (eds.), *Prophetic Religion and Politics*, New York: Paragon House, 1986, pp. 173-195.

tures; patriarchy; authoritarianism and intolerant structure of consciousness and speech. Saiedi considers the last point of great importance and amplifies it, noting the primacy of normative statements and holistic assertions; the myth of absolute knowledge and absolute values; above all, the use of authority-reference rather than rationalistic reasoning to 'prove' assertions[11].

The CCP programme of cultural management and its mode of discourse, then, seem similar in important respects to those of some other fundamentalist élites. However, particularly in the early 1960s and in the 1980s, the fundamentalist tendencies of the CCP had to contend with considerable opposition. In the first place, factions in the party have had a more critical and rational outlook than, for example, Mao in the 1970s. Marxism itself purports to abide by the norms of rational discourse, indeed to contribute to demystification. Also, industrial development was perceived as vital to the regime's survival; and the modernization programme, especially the 'opening to the west', inevitably created forces which opposed the state orthodoxy. The conflicting demands of ideological purity and technical expertise have been well known for decades.

It is hard to make a quantifiable judgement about the success or failure of the CCP in legitimizing itself and implanting new values in popular consciousness. As far as we are aware there have been no empirical studies which could offer data on this question, so one is obliged to examine more general evidence, relying on inferences from private conversations, analysis of events, and visitors' reports. The weight of evidence seems to us to point to some success in disrupting traditional values, and relative failure in instilling those advocated by the regime – certainly few people would maintain there is a wide-spread devotion to Marxism-Leninism in China which could be compared to the hold of Islam in Iran for example.

The communists strongly opposed religious beliefs, male chauvinism, feudal thinking, kinship loyalty and subordination to foreigners (cf. the 'thick ropes which bind the Chinese people'). It seems well established that all of these have suffered severe shocks since 1949, although changes in attitudes have been more profound in urban than rural areas. At the high points of collectivism and isolation from the world community, say in the late 1950s, it seemed to many that the people were throwing off old customs in accordance with Party demands. Even in the countryside women were to some extent freed from housework by communal institutions, there was an egalitarian spirit throughout most sectors of society and the patriarchal power of families was limited. Although by the 1980s many of the policies of this era had been reversed after leading to economic disaster, nonetheless things could never be quite the same again. Writers like William Hinton emphasized *fanshen*, the overthrow of traditional ways, although his daughter's return visit to Long Bow village suggested that the changes may not have been as thorough as they once appeared: about half the village had returned to Catholicism by the 1980s.

However, it seems that a clear cut alternative culture failed to arise. Perhaps this is not surprising in the countryside. By the 1980s social structures had changed

11. Ibid. pp. 189-91.

dramatically from the heyday of collectivism, which only lasted some twenty years at the maximum, despite its intensity a short period indeed in Chinese peasant life. Patriarchy, private property and kinship bonds are again determining factors in village life, and now the promotion of rural enterprises means the spread of capitalist production relations to the countryside. New industries could be more effective than ideology and collective institutions in producing a cultural transformation, but it will be a lengthy process. At present social life seems in many ways to have reverted to earlier models.

In the cities the economy has indeed been radically transformed from its pre-1949 condition, and despite the reforms of the 1980s still operates for the most part on command lines, with emphasis on bureaucratic allocation of resources, prices determined by state bureaux and quotas for production. In theory this economic system, sometimes known as 'socialism', provides the basis for a new spiritual civilization, free of exploitation and decadence, and a new system of values. The ideals most emphasized by the Party have included patriotism, dedicated service to the people, obedience to communist party leadership, honesty and incorruptibility, and at times more sinister ones such as extreme nationalism, class hatred and persecution of dissidents.

To evaluate success in implementing these ideals, we can consider three of the most important: loyalty to the regime, committed service to the people and acceptance of Marxism-Leninism. It is generally accepted that until the Cultural Revolution the urban population on the whole accepted and even supported Communist Party rule. Voices of criticism were heard in the 'hundred flowers' movement, but were confined to a very small part of the intellectual élite. However, popular support was certainly severely damaged by the Cultural Revolution and factors such as corruption, abuse of power and shortages. Spring 1989 suggested that CCP rule was ultimately based on military control and an effective security apparatus, that support for the government was ensured by fear and coercion rather than loyalty. After June 4th, reports suggest that almost the whole population of Beijing, if not other cities, harbours deep seated hatred of a regime which has become isolated, feared and tyrannical.

As to dedicated, disinterested service, two features of the 1980s which have attracted widespread media attention are corruption and materialism. Corruption has become institutionalized, no longer a matter of isolated incidents but part of the fabric of daily life. As one historian has suggested, the new movement of 'modernization' in fact spelled the revival of a whole traditional ethos – squeeze, nepotism, abuse of power. Bribery is an absolute requirement for getting things done in four very elementary aspects of social life: changing work unit, obtaining employment for one's children, obtaining housing, achieving promotion and higher pay. Ten years ago such things could be facilitated by 'presents' of alcohol or cigarettes, giving rise to the well known phrase of the early 1980s that 'those who smoke good cigarettes don't buy them, those who buy good cigarettes don't smoke them'. By 1990 the only effective measure is to leave an envelope of banknotes in the right hands. As one source told us, everybody hates it, but it is the only way to survive these days. Another side of the coin is the frenzied search for private gain in an increasingly materialist society.

Powerful government figures control access to many of the raw materials and transport facilities used in modern China's burgeoning economy, and use their control to obtain serious sums of money from industrial concerns. It seems that the Chinese people have turned to consumerism with a vengeance and that private profiteering, with nepotism and 'clanism', is far more significant than public service. The clean up of corruption was of course one of the demands made by protesters in June 1989, but government response to the problem has so far been in the realm of pronouncement rather than action[12].

As to Marxism, few Chinese regard it as anything other than a component of government domination. In particular it is a symbol of coercion over the intellectual community: artistic or research activity that appears to threaten party prestige can be labeled as anti-Marxist or unscientific, and thus censored or discredited (cf the remarks above on the fundamentalist mode of argument). Again, there must be few Chinese who sincerely believe that Marxism has any particular value as an analytical tool for understanding society, still less perhaps as a guide to a new world of harmony and social justice. It should be remembered that the Marxism which Chinese people usually encounter is quite different from the intellectually sophisticated neo-Marxism that has evolved in Europe, for example in the social sciences. Moreover, whatever its merits, Marxism as a philosophy has no intention of providing an emotional/psychological service to compete with those of traditional religions concerning such important aspects of human life as the rites of passage, the yearly festivals, coping with death.

At a more sophisticated level Marxism has relatively little to say concerning humanity's place in the cosmos, or on questions of spirituality and personal religious experience which may be of deep concern to many people. Yet it is precisely in times of social stress that people may be searching for belief systems and social institutions that offer a sense of meaning and solidarity. One of the few organizations to conduct empirical research on religion inside the PRC, the Shanghai Academy of Social Sciences, recognized this in an interesting article later translated into English[13]. Xiao notes that the majority of new believers in Shanghai are youth (people aged 18-35) and retired workers. He adduces a variety of reasons why young people may turn to religion for spiritual nourishment:

> "Many people carry spiritual wounds from the ten years of chaos, or they turn to religion for spiritual sustenance because they fail in studies or career... or because, in their view, present political or economic conditions are wrong... Among some youthful new believers the influence of Western culture has had a definite role... There are also some people who are dissatisfied with the mores of society... some have nothing to do in their spare time."

12. Graphic details of corruption in the PRC have been reported in the *Far Eastern Economic Review*, and also in T.B. Gold, "After Comradeship: Personal Relations in China since the Cultural Revolution", *China Quarterly*, no 104, December 1985, pp. 657-675.
13. Xiao Zhitian, "Some Opinions on Present Religious Phenomena" in *Ching Feng*, vol 26, no 4, December 1983, pp.212- 221. A collection of papers on religion by staff of the Shanghai Academy of Social Sciences, edited by Luo Zhufeng, will shortly be published in translation by Donald MacInnis.

His observations on retired workers seem particularly sharp:

> "Many, with nowhere to while away the empty hours after retirement, go everyday to the parks...where they exercise and stroll and chat. Their cultural level is low and they are easily moved by those who would preach to them, despite the fact that they do not understand the mysteries of theology. They are deeply attracted by the pious atmosphere of the churches and temples and become enthusiastic believers. Quite a few people with chronic diseases or senility...seek help through prayer or recitation of Buddhist scripture, burning incense and worshiping Buddha. If they get spiritual and psychological comfort in this way, they believe even more strongly that they have received the protection of God or Buddha[14]."

The re-emergence of religion, then, in the cities at least, may be linked with a deep scepticism concerning official ideology, and a failure on the part of the government to maintain genuine popular support. Students, intellectuals, workers in a variety of professions and retired people may be disillusioned or never interested in a Marxism which is closely identified with a totalitarian regime. Many of them may be potentially interested in religion as an alternative. Yet it is in the cities that government control is strongest, and religious groups must find some accommodation with the regime in order to survive.

Accommodation - Religions in an Atheist State

In the early 1950s the CCP demanded the formation of 'Patriotic Associations' to act as official representatives of the major religions in China. The most important were the China Buddhist Association, the China Catholic Patriotic Association and the (Protestant) Three Self Patriotic Movement (TSPM). These organizations have played a central role in Chinese religious life. We do not intend to give here a resume of their development nor of state policy on religion since there are detailed accounts by several authors[15]. The formation of these organizations and the exclusion of foreign missionaries should be placed in the context of CCP strategy to eliminate western influence in the early years of the People's Republic[16].

Here we will offer some reflections concerning the role of such organizations in Chinese political life and the implications this may have for believers. Unfortunately there is not space to elucidate the historical background. It should, however, be noted that CCP policy is not only an expression of Leninist hostility to religion. At least since the Tang dynasty the Chinese state insisted on

14. Xiao, ibid., p. 217.
15. For example, Welch, op. cit; Wickeri, op. cit; and Kim-Kwong Chan, *Towards a Contextual Ecclesiology: the Catholic Church in the PRC, 1979-83. Its Life and Theological Implications*, Hong Kong: Phototech Systems Ltd., 1987.
16. See B. Hooper, *China Stands Up: Ending the Western Presence 1948-1950*, London: Allen and Unwin, 1986.

imposing controls over all religions in China, sometimes using mechanisms strikingly similar to those adopted by the CCP[17].

We start from the perspective that a major priority of the CCP has been to maintain control over all sectors of society by a variety of strategies ranging from manipulation to coercion. The demand from believers has been for a space in society in which they can practice their religions without persecution. This contrast of interests has led to the negotiation of an area of legality, the centre of which is understood and accepted by most parties, but the edges of which shade off into various grey patches of illegality, clandestinity and conflict.

The theoretical basis for CCP co-operation with non-communist groupings is the 'united front', an important analysis of which is made by van Slyke[18]. The CCP had allied temporarily with the Guomindang in its early years and under Mao adopted united front tactics in the 1930s and 1940s. The composition of the united front changed according to the tactical requirements of the situation, but the underlying intention was to ally with a broad spectrum of the population at any one time in order to isolate and overcome the enemy. In the 1940s, for example, the CCP declared that as representative of the proletariat it could unite with poor and middle peasants, the urban petty and national bourgeoisie and various other 'patriotic elements'. The intention was to isolate those who sided with imperialists, feudalists and the Guomindang.

Judgements on the sincerity of the united front policy tend to reflect writers' overall assessment of the communist government. For some it has basically been a success, only marred by periods of aberration like the Cultural Revolution. Wickeri, who tends to this perspective, summarizes three aspects of the united front as: learning from others; consultation; concern for the people's well-being. He suggests that 'the united front is a consensus-building approach that seeks to create a unified political standpoint' and that 'democratic consultation' is an important feature of its day-to-day working[19]. He also gives a useful account of the organizational structure of the united front mass organizations, 'transmission belts' as Jean Chesneaux referred to them: they are supposed to explain and win support for decisions from above, and make known the concrete problems and feelings of those below. The process is overseen by the United Front Work Department, a party body that has had great importance in implementing policy with regard to religious questions. It is probably true that

17. Several writers have noticed a formal symmetry between Imperial and Communist state policy on religion: State orthodoxy, tolerated and registered heterodoxies and marginal sects. However we believe this may also mask the extent to which the communist state has broken with tradition. Its ideology has roots in nineteenth century European scientism and comparisons with the Imperial tradition need to be made with some care. A discussion of this can be found in C.K. Yang, *Religion in Chinese Society*, Berkeley: University of California Press, 1961, and in Jonathan Chao (ed.), *Zhongguo dui jidujiao de zhengce* (China's Policy towards Christianity), Hong Kong: Chinese Church Research Center, 1983. See also Kim-Kwong Chan "A Chinese Perspective on the Interpretation of the Chinese Government's Religious Policy" in the present volume.
18. L.P. van Slyke, *Enemies and Friends: the United Front in Chinese Communist History*, Stanford: Stanford University Press, 1967.
19. Wickeri, op. cit., pp. 60-61.

the Department has at times worked conscientiously to promote the interests of minority groups, but, as Wickeri notes, it has also paid great attention to surveillance, control and security.

Others make a more negative assessment. Van Slyke, for example, suggests that in practice the united front slogan became an empty formula after the communists took power, covering a nominal participation in political life by various minority groups while reserving all policy and executive powers in the hands of the CCP. He concludes that is has become a component of communist leaders' self-image, reflecting their need to see themselves as presiding over a happy united nation. Chinese popular speech reflects a similar opinion in the colloquial term for the non-communist organizations represented in the political process: *huapingdang*, flower vase parties, used for strictly decorative purposes. A more sinister aspect of the united front is the tendency to draw a line, at CCP leaders' convenience, between 'friends' and 'enemies'. As noted earlier, the latter can be treated as heretics, unworthy of being accorded basic human rights. The political rhetoric of united front ideology has sometimes been used to justify mass persecutions.

Here we feel it is again useful to turn to the Soviet Union for a comparison which may yield insights into the development of the 'united front' approach. Van Slyke suggests that in China it became largely symbolic; an interesting paper by K. Jowitt provides a different perspective. Jowitt suggests that once they have consolidated power, Leninist parties may need to devise new institutions to mediate between themselves and other interest groups. A wide range of social élites are admitted to consultative status in sociopolitical activities. In this way new forces are co-opted into the control apparatus but power remains with the party[20].

Jowitt identifies various benefits and dangers arising from this policy. The regime can rely on manipulation and persuasion rather than coercion; problems can be approached more critically and pragmatically, there can be more emphasis on merit and procedural criteria. The techniques of cultural management identified by Lane, such as political/religious ceremonies, are an example of this kind of manipulation. On the other hand, imposition of authority becomes more complex, as more people need to be consulted, ideological consent is diluted, and at least passive resistance may occur at relatively senior levels. 'Inclusion' of this kind has been an important strategy in China, for example the enrolment of successful businessmen in the CCP in the mid-1980s, although alternating with purges to strengthen ideological commitment. It has been very apparent in religion: since the early 1950s all religious movements have been obliged to produce leaders who are willing to work in national organizations which support government policy and conform to government demands. This phenomenon, which can be seen in the case of Buddhists, Protestants, Catholics and Taoists (the popular religious traditions being somewhat different), leads to many interesting questions.

20. K. Jowitt, "Inclusion and Mobilization in European Leninist Regimes", in *World Politics*, October 1975, pp. 69-96.

In the first place, in relatively liberal years, for example 1979-89, believers enrolled in the national associations have not generally suffered persecution. They can practise their beliefs and even achieve notable social consolidation, for example the restoration of confiscated property and the establishment of training schools. Leaders have been able to travel abroad, to develop research and training, to debate religious beliefs, and above all to find their religion a place in the surrounding civil society. They win ground for their followers in a concrete, practical manner, affording protection against arbitrary repression and achieving some measure of legitimacy. The activities of these organizations are relatively well known outside China since they have attracted the support of many groups in Europe, the USA and Japan.

Their views are to be found expounded in the various official publications, the most significant of which are *Tianfeng* (Protestant), *Fayin* (Buddhist) and *Zhongguo tianzhujiao* (Catholic). The journals reflect the political line that is required by current policy: support for party leadership, encouragement to join in social programmes such as the four modernizations, hard work and good citizenship. However these issues do not dominate the content of the journals, only a small proportion of which relates directly to political issues. The remainder is concerned with the religious questions that are, one suspects, of greater interest to most of the readers. The political content acts as a concession that lends the journals protection without seriously damaging their credibility[21].

Such religious leaders, then, decided to co-operate more or less unreservedly with state power. They achieved a measure of legality and even power for their organizations, international recognition, restoration of property and a likelihood of continuity in the context of Chinese society as it moves into the 1990s. From the point of view of millions of believers all over China these were major successes that made the 1980s their most peaceful, fruitful decade since 'liberation'. The ordinary believer was not asked to compromise him or herself by political deals, the burden of which was shouldered by a relatively small number of leaders. The great benefit this brought to ordinary believers was that they could engage in religious activities openly and legally, without having to risk political trouble. This much tends to be admitted, if grudgingly, even by leaders of fundamentalist groups opposed to the 'patriotic associations'.

good pt.

However, everything has its price. A consequence of this strategy is that religious organizations become discredited in some circles. Many of those turning to religion are doing so because they are not satisfied with what the state has to offer. Looking for an alternative, they cannot find one in organizations which perforce praise government policy in almost every sphere of life. Official religion has essentially renounced social criticism. Occasional complaints are made by religious leaders about local harassment, but these are couched in language which emphasizes that the national leadership is not to blame: the usual approach is to argue that local officials have contravened a more liberal policy

21. However a detailed analysis would certainly reveal changes in doctrine to accommodate with CCP demands. See for example Buddhist leaders' efforts to justify class struggle in 'Interpreting Buddhist Doctrine', Welch, op. cit., Chapter Eight.

decided at national level. Beyond that, sermons, articles and interviews tend to have a similar flavour: whenever political or social issues are raised, the response is exhortation to obey party leadership and to co-operate wholeheartedly with the authorities. For example, *Tianfeng* published many reports of support for government action on June 4th, expressing approval of the repression of rebellion and solidarity with the martial law troops. The position bears resemblances to that of the Church in early Soviet Russia. According to Hosking, in 1927 a leader of the Orthodox church proclaimed:

> "We wish to be Orthodox believers, and at the same time to acknowledge the Soviet Union as our civil motherland, whose joys and successes are our joys and successes, and whose misfortunes are our misfortunes." Asked privately how he could accept such a humiliating predicament he replied: "We must preserve the Church for the people: after that the Lord will show us what we must do[22]."

This strategy is comparable to that of Chinese church leaders. However in the Gorbachev era different aspects of the policy became evident. For example, it appeared that opponents to Stalinist rule had scant respect for those who had co-operated. Orthodox leaders, who may indeed have kept the flame of religious belief alight through desperate years, may also have compromised themselves irredeemably in the eyes of those who for years suffered the consequences of opposition on human rights and other issues. On the other hand, religious groups who had operated in clandestinity, subject to persecution for decades, at last felt able to come into the open. There are accounts of tremendous popular enthusiasm for the illegal Catholic Church in Ukraine, while 'reform Baptists', who staged the first unofficial public demonstration for forty years in 1966, have attained almost heroic status as long term, populist, purist opponents of the state[23].

It would not be difficult to draw comparisons with China. If there was a profound shake up of the system, with liberalization and pluralism of the political scene, one indeed wonders how much credibility and support would be accorded to the leaders of the various pro-government organizations that have steadfastly refused to comment on, much less criticize, any aspect of communist rule. It is understandable that one should not breathe a word of criticism for the June 4th massacre: one might well be imprisoned and many hard earned concessions would be jeopardized. But by not doing so one certainly becomes identified with the official line that government action was justifiable self-defence. Leaders must feel in an impossible dilemma: to survive through compromise – some would say collaboration – or to court destruction. A leading Chinese dissident in exile, Liu Binyan, made a remark at a recent conference which illustrates the point. Asked what he thought about a certain church leader, Liu Binyan said that he did not know much about him. In a rather disparaging tone he continued:

22. G. Hosking, "The Atheist State", in *the Listener* vol 120 no 3092, 8 December 1988, p. 5.
23. Ibid., p.7.

"The main thing these religious leaders do after any social disturbances is to run to the authorities and say "Don't blame us – there are no dissidents in our organization!"

Pye has noted that the lack of profound, penetrating social criticism is a pervasive weakness in Chinese society. The most that is permitted is complaint, which is somehow seen as within the bounds of loyal subservience. When complaint extends to analysis of causes it cannot be tolerated, as discovered by Wei Jingsheng and other radical critics[24]. Religious groups have seldom indulged in complaints, let alone social analysis: and political attitude must of course profoundly influence the type of religion that is propounded. At one extreme it may become a blessing on the state, a celebration of temporal leaders however corrupt, and this has earned some religious groups the popular epithet of *fanshipai*, those who endorse everything. Surely a great gulf opens here between political expediency and personal feelings. Perhaps the one alleviating factor in this whole difficult situation is the traditional Chinese tolerance of public conformity and private disagreement, which may make the situation somewhat less stressful than it would be for westerners. King and Bond, reporting sociopsychological studies on Chinese culture, write:

"Chinese conformity . . . is often nothing more than surface conformity, that is, compliance without internalization... Chinese persons are not subject to the same pressures for consistency between inner beliefs and outer behaviour as are Westerners... One generally responds to the dictates of the situation rather than to the dictates of one's self. Such behaviour is not construed as hypocritical or insincere as it would be by Westerners; in a way it is a culturally sanctioned mechanism enabling the individual to maintain a harmonious relationship with the outside world[25]."

The authors also stress, however, that they do not subscribe to the view that the Chinese character is inherently or unconditionally submissive. On the contrary even the Confucian tradition, not to mention less official views, allows nonconformism in some circumstances, for example to overthrow tyrannical leaders who have exceeded the bounds of legitimacy. The reservation of private opinion may be the only realistic alternative where open rebellion would simply be smashed. In Thomas Gold's interesting article on personal relations in China he reports the following:

"As one man explained to me, there was a distinct subtext to all interactions. An object of the proletarian dictatorship, he was especially sensitive to signals

24. Lucian W. Pye, *The Mandarin and the Cadre: China's Political Culture*, Ann Arbor: University of Michigan, 1988.
25. A.Y.C. King and M.H. Bond, "The Confucian Paradigm of Man: a Sociological View", in D. Y. H. Yu (ed.), *Chinese Culture and Mental Health*, Orlando, Florida: Academic Press, 1985, p. 35.

about what behaviour was expected of him – how to act (*biaoxian*) in any given situation. When he passed the leading cadre in his unit, the safest ploy was to recite the current slogan. 'I knew I didn't believe what I said' the man informed me, 'and the cadre knew I didn't believe it either, and I knew he knew I didn't believe it, but as long as I said it, it was sufficient to get me through the interaction[26]."

Writ large, this seems a fair description of methods adopted by institutional religions in the PRC. Perhaps the most subtle and complex analysis along these lines is that made by Holmes Welch[27]. Buddhist leaders were used to rally Buddhists behind domestic programmes and to support initiatives in foreign policy, for example the exclusion of Taiwan from international organizations. To assure complete dependence on the state, Buddhist associations, journals and monasteries were obliged to operate strictly under government guidance and on official subsidies. However, this inevitably served the purposes of Buddhists too. There was the rub:

"No matter how carefully the government dispensed its patronage to religious groups, it kept them in being. A monastery that had been repaired as an architectural monument and had monks living in it to impress visitors from Southeast Asia was – in terms of religious practice – more alive than one that had been converted into a police station. *Modern Buddhism* [an official Buddhist journal] did useful work in transmitting directives and study materials to Buddhists, but in order to qualify as their journal it also had to publish articles that presented, however abstractly or distortedly, Buddhist doctrines. The CBA [China Buddhist Association] was the agent of the government in dealing with Buddhists at home and abroad, but its very existence gave a certain legitimacy to Buddhism. Thus the short-term program to utilize Buddhism conflicted with the long-term program to let it die of its own accord. What made matters worse was the ingenuity of Buddhists in using a wide variety of official policies and campaigns as a screen behind which they could carry on traditional religious activities[28]."

Welch gives accounts of the latter which would be amusing were the issues not so grave. For example in 1950 a large group of Buddhists came together in Peking to uphold world peace in the face of American imperialism. For seven days they chanted liturgy and expounded sutras to the delight of large audiences. Welch asks how this is to be interpreted:

"Had the People's Government succeeded in using Buddhists for its own purposes – in whipping up an anti-American campaign? Or was it the other way round – had Buddhists used the peace movement as the screen behind which they could chant and lecture on the sutras to large gatherings of the faithful just as they always had done in the past[29]?"

26. Gold, op. cit., p. 668.
27. Welch, op. cit.
28. Ibid., p. 258.
29. Ibid., p. 259.

The institutional religions, then, are caught in a complex of moral, political and religious dilemmas. Few would deny that their leaders have won substantial and important concessions for believers, on the other hand many would argue that too high a price has been paid. At the other extreme of the political spectrum is the voice of prophetic Christianity. From the 1950s some religious leaders regarded the communist authorities as fundamentally anti-religious, and argued that despite short term benefits, negotiation with them was tantamount to moral suicide. Hundreds of religious figures who refused to deal with the national organizations ended in concentration camps, achieving a moral purity at the expense of political survival. Among the most famous of these is Wang Mingdao, whose religious convictions led him to labour camps for over twenty years. He has been criticized for an isolationist, rejectionist stance vis-a-vis the secular authorities. It could also be said that he and others kept alive a different aspect of religion: not the institutions, but the spirit which refuses to be silenced.

The picture that emerges of 'offical' religion, as one would expect, mirrors many of the themes in Chinese society. Many people, perhaps disillusioned with official ideology, turn to religion in a 'quiet' way, maintaining normal social practices and avoiding conflict with the authorities, being flexible and discreet. However, in a large number of cases, there seems to be a more radical dimension to Chinese religious life – adherence to sects and secret organizations which operate in conflict with goverment requirements. The latter have probably been more influential in the countryside or minor provincial towns, to which we now turn.

Popular Religion – Beyond the Boundaries

A recurrent feature of Chinese studies has been an excessive attention on the culture of the élite, who produced most of the documents and were in other respects more accessible to historians. However, it is of vital importance to correct this bias by serious study of 'the world beyond the boundaries of the ruling class[30]'. It is necessary in this context to examine religion among the rural population and among less affluent sectors of the urban masses. Yet this certainly entails difficulties. Very few empirical studies exist, the government is not keen to promote further research, the population concerned is vast, and this kind of religion generates fewer written documents. Moreover the situation is probably one of rapid change. Given these factors, for the present it will only be possible to make some general observations.

We have suggested that rural as well as urban Chinese have seen far reaching changes in this generation. Some peasants may be deeply disturbed by the new experiences of the past decade and want to hold to traditional beliefs, expressed in time-honoured ceremonies and practices; others are uprooted, finding them-

30. D. Johnson, A.J. Nathan and E.S. Rawski (eds.), *Popular Culture in Late Imperial China*, Berkeley: University of California Press, 1985, ix.

selves in completely new social environments as the first generation of immigrants to cities. They may turn to new religions to achieve some sense of identity in group activity, reconstructing a new community to replace the damaged kinship network, perhaps turning to fundamentalist beliefs for simple, monocausal explanations for the complex changes taking place in their lives. In this and the next section we will briefly consider two aspects, which one suspects may often co-exist: the revival of tradition and adherence to new sects.

The study of Chinese popular religions has given rise to various theoretical perspectives, many of which are analyzed in a review article by Catherine Bell, who examines the various implicit assumptions and practical ramifications of views held on fundamental concepts such as culture, religion and tradition in the field of Chinese studies, notably anthropology[31]. On the practical level it is noteworthy that most of the empirical studies are based in Taiwan and Hong Kong, presumably for reasons of access – this is the case, for example, with all the papers in the valuable collection *Religion and Ritual in Chinese Society*[32]. The important historical studies of popular and sectarian religion in China itself rarely move beyond 1900[33]. These studies are therefore useful for purposes of comparison, to see how Chinese communities have developed in other societies, but may have limited relevance in explaining changes on the mainland, which were surely influenced by forty years of communist government. Some observers have tended to downplay the impact of the government and instead insisted on the resilience of popular culture[34], but it would be difficult to maintain that the continuous pressure of state policy over forty years has had no effect whatsoever. Support for the contention that government policy can have an important impact on popular religion comes from Watson's paper 'Standardizing the Gods' which demonstrates how profoundly government guidelines influenced the Tian Hou cult in South China[35].

There are many reports, fragmentary but cumulative, of the widespread practice of popular religion in China today, for example the following from Stephan Feuchtwang:

31. C. Bell, "Religion and Chinese Culture: towards an Assessment of 'Popular Religion' ", in *History of Religions*, Summer 1989.
32. A. Wolf (ed.), *Religion and Ritual in Chinese Society*, Stanford: Stanford University Press, 1974. This exclusive focus on Taiwan and Hong Kong, although understandable, can lead to lack of obsevation concerning the PRC. For example, A.P. Cohen, writing as late as 1987, ("Chinese Popular Religion" in M. Eliade (ed.) *Encyclopedia of Religion*, vol 3, New York: MacMillan, 1987, pp. 289-296), states, in an otherwise masterly account of Chinese popular religion, that popular traditions have virtually disappeared in the PRC as a result of government policy.
33. For example S. Naquin, "The Transmission of White Lotus Sectarianism in Late Imperial China", in D. Johnson et al. (eds), op. cit; D.L. Overmyer, *Folk Buddhist Religion: Dissenting Sects in Late Traditional China*, Cambridge, Mass.: Harvard University Press, 1976.
34. See I.W. Mabbett, *Modern China: the Mirage of Modernity*, Beckenham: Croom Helm, 1985.
35. L.J. Watson. "Standardizing the Gods: the Promotion of T'ien Hou ("Empress of Heaven") along the South China Coast, 960-1960", in D. Johnson et al, op. cit.

"Being permanent and recognisable structures, temples are observable at any time and to a passing scan from the fastest road transport. I traveled thus, eyes pealed around Xiamen and Quanzhou in southern Fujian and was surprised to see even more temples than I had been led to expect. True this was a relatively wealthy part of the province compared with counties further inland. But every small town or administrative village through which I passed had a small temple. In the warm south moreover the front rooms of houses and small shops are often open to the street. In about one in four of those that were open during a walk around part of Xiamen city, domestic altars with incense burners and figures of gods could be seen. In two nearby villages on the day of Qing Ming, when ancestors are honoured and graves cleaned, residents laid offerings on tables in front rooms and burned spirit money outside their doors unabashed by a visitor and uncensored by accompanying officials[36]."

One should be careful before generalizing from this observation. Xiamen and its surrounding area is allowed an unusual degree of freedom to please the large numbers of overseas Chinese who return there. Tolerance is the price paid to attract foreign currency. Nevertheless it seems likely that such activities are allowed to continue in many areas if they are kept low key. However, sometimes they overstep the boundaries of local tolerance, when they are usually denounced as 'feudal superstitions' and often disrupted by arrests of leading participants. Many hundreds of reports such as the following have appeared in the Chinese press in the past decade:

"From 13.00 on August 21 to 02.00 on August 22nd 1989, the public security bureau of Shouning county [Fuzhou] was surrounded and wrecked by a group of peasants who conducted activities based on feudal superstition... These people who conducted superstitious activities came from more than twenty... villages... and numbered over 1,000. They were escorting the Tongtian Shengmu back to her shrine yesterday morning. When they passed through the county seat, cadres and policemen of the public security organ, together with personnel of the armed police corps, tried twice to dissuade and stop the procession[37]."

In general, such 'feudal superstitions' are only reported in the press when they occasion public disorder or provoke the authorities in some way. Presumably such incidents are few compared to those that pass off witout trouble, and one can only assume that there is in the 1980s widespread participation in popular religious activities over much of rural China. From the fragmentary reports available it seems that the 'superstitious activities' are derived from popular religion as practised before 1949 and similar to that practised in Hong Kong and Taiwan (for the southern provinces at least). One would expect them to centre

36. Feuchtwang, op. cit., p. 77.
37. From the BBC *Summary of World Broadcasts*, Parts 3: The Far East, (FE0421). Many other accounts of popular religious activities can be traced through the indices to this publication.

around the trinity of 'gods, ghosts and ancestors' with different aspects emphasized in different districts, a strong emphasis on pragmatism and practice rather than doctrine, and a reinforcement of traditional social patterns such as exogamy and patriarchy. Borrowing a metaphor from computing, these traditions acted as a kind of 'default setting' in popular culture: individuals would tend to follow local traditions unless there were special reasons for them not to. Each community would have its own particular combination of deities and its own methods of propitiation and supplication.

One of the most deeply rooted attractions was the promise of help in times of sickness, childbirth, death and other critical periods. Potter reports that Cantonese villagers attribute most children's illnesses to 'soul loss', believing that children are vulnerable to attack from malicious spirits and ghosts. One means of protecting a weak child, or curing a sick one, is to employ a shaman, who will summon a benificent deity to help. Shamans are also needed for certain adult ailments and to propitiate angry ancestors who may be damaging prosperity and health[38]. Given that in the 1980s health care in most remote parts of China is primitive, or expensive, or both, it is not surprising that many peasants still turn to traditional health providers. The re-instatement of traditional forms of social organization in the countryside, i.e. the return to family farming, has perhaps encouraged the return of traditional forms of religious practice. We have no access to systematic data, but Stephen Endicott provides a detailed account of the shift in villagers' attitudes in the course of the 1980s reforms which suggests this may be so[39].

One informant who lived until recently in Guangdong province reported that in his opinion the revival in popular religious practices in the 1980s was the result not so much of more relaxed government policy as of the break up of collective farming. He agreed that there had been fierce penalties for 'feudal superstition' during the Cultural Revolution, but stated that in the villages he knew the peasants would have practised it anyway had they been so inclined. In his view the important change was that while the communes existed, each family felt far less responsible for its own well being, both in health and money matters. If a problem arose, the usual response was to approach the brigade or commune leaders and request assistance. However unsatisfactory the situation, it was felt that answers could and should be provided by the collective. Conversely, after the revival of family farming, there was little help to be had from such institutions and people soon began to turn to religious specialists for help, advice or comfort. In Noverber 1989 the government announced that 'feudal superstition' was on its list of 'Six vices' which will be the targets of a new campaign (the others include prostitution, gambling and pornography). Perhaps it will then be possible to determine whether administrative hostility can in fact dampen this tradition in the social context of small peasant farming communities.

On the positive side, adherents of a neo-Durkheimian analysis might argue that popular religious practices provide a sense of colour, celebration, community

38. J.M. Potter, "Cantonese Shamanism" in A. Wolf, op. cit., p. 222ff.
39. S. Endicott, *Red Earth: Revolution in a Sichuan Village*, London: I.B. Tauris, 1988.

solidarity, folk art, social cement and cultural identity - some of the benefits that have been theorized as accruing from such traditions. The enthusiasm with which they are embraced suggest that such activities do indeed have a deep root in people's hearts. Of course some observers have been concerned to point out darker sides of the picture - for example Lu Hsun in the famous short story 'Medicine' which depicts a family gripped by superstition and ignorance - while others have deplored the resources spent on these 'unproductive' activities. Feuchtwang concludes that in general, as far as officials are concerned, 'popular religion is simply a sign of backwardness' the answer to which is improvement of education and culture[40]. He suggests that Chinese academics are unlikely to undertake the task of elucidating further the role of popular religion in the sociology of popular culture and ethnicity, unless changes in government priorities call for it. Whether non-Chinese will pursue the matter remains to be seen.

The Reincarnation of Sectarianism

A relatively new phenomenon is the growth of evangelical Christianity, reports of which have come from many parts of China. This seems to cause some embarrassment to the government, and not least to the leaders of official bodies such as the Three Self Movement who are confronted with the spread of heterodox teachings by itinerant evangelists. Even worse, this kind of Christianity seems to have support from abroad (particularly from agencies in Hong Kong and the USA), to resonate with traditional peasant concerns of exorcism and healing, and to refuse co-operation with the state apparatus. News of this movement is fragmentary and unsatisfactory. Moreover almost all reports emanate from evangelical sources in Hong Kong which would probably tend to exaggerate the importance of the phenomenon. On the other hand it would probably be unwise to discount such reports: after all, the official church news sources also have a political position to maintain and are also unlikely to be entirely accurate.

While reserving some scepticism, it is interesting to note the claims of evangelical sources, here taken from a book by Paul Kauffman, a missionary, researcher and journalist with more than fifty years experience of China. Based on information received in Hong Kong, Kauffman maintains that government studies deliberately underestimate the growth of Christianity, sometimes by huge amounts. Quoting internal Pubic Security statistics, he maintains that of Christian converts in Xian, only two per cent had been baptized and received as members in the official Church. The other 98 per cent had all been converted through the witness of independent house church evangelists. The official statistics of the TSPM are only the tip of the iceberg.[41]

40. Feuchtwang, op. cit., p. 85.
41. P.E. Kauffman, *Piecing Together the China Puzzle*, Hong Kong: Asian Outreach, 1987, p. 89. The term TSPM (Three Self Patriotic Movement) refers to the official church's national political organization.

Kauffman claims rapid Church growth in Henan in particular, where the TSPM has only a tenuous foothold. In Kaifeng ten per cent of the population are Christians, while in Fangcheng county, which local cadres have dubbed a 'Jesus nest', approximately half are. Kauffman puts the number of believers in Henan alone at around ten million, compared to the official estimate of 600,000. While it is not possible to confirm the statistics offered by either party, it is at least important to note that such striking discrepancies exist. Equally striking discrepancies exist in the interpretation of the motives and archievements of institutionalized religious movements such as the TSPM. Kauffman's views are quite at odds with those of the official church, allegedly reflecting the position of house church leaders who oppose the TSPM: the top official leaders are more Marxist than Christian, they are willing tools of the CCP, they do not believe in scripture, they oppose evangelism, in short:

> "We consider the TSPM to be an espionage organization that exists to spy on people and report them to the civil authorities and cause their arrest... In 1983 several hundred believers in our area were arrested. It was representatives of the TSPM that put the finger on us and caused our arrest, like Judas did. When we were eventually brought up in court it was the TSPM representatives that were our accusers[42]."

At one end of the spectrum, evangelical Christianity is apparently close to orthodoxy, and many groups of 'house church' Christians co-operate easily with the TSPM. However at the opposite end, it seems that these popular groups blend in with the more traditional Chinese environment, and elements such as exorcism, healing and supernatural powers are prominent in their practices. It seems that many people are attracted to some form of Christianity, but are not overseen by professional pastors or strongly influenced by official church publications. Until very recently even Bibles were very scarce in many rural areas and the understanding of the Christian message must have been very different from that of urban intellectuals.

This aspect of Christianity in China arouses mixed reactions. Wickeri calls the phenomenon "folk Protestantism" and calls it "a problem", regretting that it will "continue to pose problems to social order in the Chinese countryside". For him this "underscores the urgent need for theological training and more effective pastoral leadership[43]." Bob Whyte regrets the kinds of confusion that could arise from the sects, giving examples of people who claimed to be reincarnations of Jesus, exploiting gullible followers. He is particularly sharp with outsiders who presume to encourage such sects, sometimes advocating confrontational tactics leading to violence. Whyte is sensitive to the reasons for unregistered groups, but concludes his discussion:

42. Kauffman, op. cit., p. 110, allegedly citing statements by house church leaders.
43. Wickeri, op. cit., p. 284.

Good – polarized portrayal of sectarian Xtians

"The rapid spread of such a heterodox movement shows the vulnerability of the home meetings when they are not a part of a wider church structure. Sudden and speedy growth without effective organization is bound to lead to problems. Untrained and often self-selected leaders can lead to the espousal of a whole range of heresies and to the domination of groups by people with their own hidden agendas[44]."

Again, a very different view is given by supporters of these groups, who present them in a rather romantic light as martyrs, rebels, saints, blessed. Again taking Kauffman as representative of this trend, Chapter Ten of his book, entitled "Preachers on the Run – Risking Life and Limb for the Gospel", gives glowing accounts of "traveling servants of the Lord" who constantly risk arrest and imprisonment:

"[They] choose not to allow the TSPM to constrain their calling... They have been called of God to reach the unreached and that is what the Party does not want to happen[45]".

This atmosphere of mystery and miracles can be explored at length in publications put out by Hong Kong based groups such as Asia Outreach and Chinese Communications. It seems likely that Buddhism also shades off into this area of popular religiosity but so far we have come across no documentary evidence, although Whyte quotes two instances where Buddhist elements have been incorporated into Christianity[46].

The influx of evangelists from Hong Kong and the prestige of western countries may have contributed to the growth in Christianity, whose symbols and religious language speak powerfully to Chinese peasants at present. However it is important to note that other forms of sectarian religion have also spread in the 1980s. Sectarianism in China dates back at least to the Song dynasty and has a complex history. The sects tend to evolve complex patterns of belief and religious practice, drawing on Buddhism, Taoism and Confucianism. They usually worship a mother goddess as well as a varied pantheon of heroes, and often practise vegetarianism, meditation, martial arts or spirit writing. Millenarianism is often an important component of their belief systems.

OK

The role of religion in rural dissent in Qing China has been documented by Overmyer, who explains that these religious groups should not be identified with the secret societies, although confusion is easy because the latter often adopted clourful rituals from religions, particularly Buddhism. However, the religious sects were primarily evangelical, not esoteric: they were geared to the long term practice of religion in peace time, not to the life of political rebellion[47].

44. R. Whyte, *Unfinished Encounter: China and Christianity*, London: Collins, 1988, p. 408.
45. Kauffman, op. cit., p. 128.
46. Whyte, op. cit., p. 411.
47. Overmyer, op. cit., pp. 55-70.

For many centuries these sects have played an important role in China's religious culture, and at times have impinged on the political scene. A Public Security Bureau document from 1985 expresses anxiety about the rapid resurgence of sectarianism in the 1980s: "some sects such as the *yiguandao* extend to virtually every area of the land and have extremely large memberships[48]". Two American scholars have recently suggested that evangelical Christianity has similarities with these sects which perhaps contribute to its popularity.

Daniel Bays notes that Christianity might not be seen by Chinese primarily as a foreign religion. In its social functions and beliefs it displays significant parallels to a range of heterodox sects. For example, almost all sectarians believed in a creator deity and in some form of salvation. They tended to be egalitarian and emphasized self-improvement and morality. The congregation was the typical form of organization, with local charismatic leaders playing an important role. Liturgy, reading of scriptures, preaching, offering money and communal meals were important practices. Family and lineage ties were important in conversion patterns[49].

Murray Rubinstein, who has mostly worked on Christianity in Taiwan, takes up this theme and proposes the importance of 'congruence' between existing and new religious ideas. It is much easier to transmit a new religion if the missionary can establish the existence of key parallel cultural patterns and structures. He may then convince his audience that though his religion at first sight is new and strange, in fact it is an improvement on existing beliefs and practices rather than a total rejection of them. An example is the True Jesus Church teaching that the Holy Spirit enters into Christian believers at prayer. This is easily accepted by those who already believe in local shamans or *tong khi*. 'True Jesus theologians... are quick to argue that *tong khi* are inhabited by evil spirits... while those individuals within their church... are possessed by the Holy Spirit[50]'. There is no attempt to deny the phenomenon of possession, rather to co-opt it into the new belief. Christianity is in a complex position in China. In the eyes of the politically sophisticated it was inextricably linked with foreign domination in the nineteenth century, and there are still suspicions about loyalty to foreign powers - notably of course the Vatican. On the other hand it probably benefits from the present high prestige of western capitalism and, as just suggested, perhaps is less strange to Chinese people than it might appear at first sight.

Finally, it is interesting to note that pentecostal and charismatic Christianity has also grown markedly in Taiwan in the past decade, as well as in countries as far apart as Korea, Brazil and South Africa. Important elements of the faith are the absolute authority of scripture, personal salvation by grace, dedication and commitment, and a heavy stress on evangelism. Pentecostalists believe in the direct and active intervention of the Holy Spirit and typically claim that their

48. Quoted in *Chinese Sociology and Anthropology*, Vol 21, Summer 1989, p. 3.
49. D.H. Bays, "Christianity and the Chinese Sectarian Tradition" in *Ch'ing-shih Went'i*, vol 4 no 7, 1982, pp. 33-55.
50. M.A. Rubinstein, "Taiwan's Churches of the Holy Spirit" in *The American Asian Review*, vol 6 no 3, Fall 1988, p. 47.

churches represent a return to the First Century Christian experience. They also attach great importance to the phenomena of glossolalia (speaking in tongues) and spiritual healing. It will be noted that these are all reported as important aspects of folk protestantism in China, although how much the reporting is distorted is hard to say.

The phenomenon is discussed briefly in a paper by the Taiwanese scholar Yih-yuan Li, who proposes that rituals can be considered symptoms of group reaction under the stresses of social change, notably the rapid industrialization of Taiwan and migration to the cities of its rural population. For lonely and anxious newcomers, "religious faith and participation is undoubtedly a mechanism for adjustment... they tend to join religious sects that have overtones of anti-ritualism... prefer direct contact with God and go into a trance easily[51]".

Li notes the importance of bodily dissociation – trances, trembling, shaking, glossolalia – as a reflection of the fragmentation of their social world. In a sense every member of the congregation who is able to experience such phenomena becomes a kind of shaman, participating in a mode of consciousness away from the cares of everyday existence. Li notes that group shamanistic cults are now becoming popular in Taiwan's urban centres and these display notable parallels to Christian pentecostalist churches. Li also notes that a major difference lies in the exclusive attitude of the Christians who tend to denounce other sects as agents of Satan while maintaining that they themselves are filled with Holy Spirit.

It may be difficult to discover where and why evangelical Christianity has taken root in China for lack of empirical evidence. Certainly it would not be surprising if it were among groups experiencing social disruption, if it appealed to minorities of various kinds, new migrants, women, dispossessed peasants. It would seem to have a congruity with elements of traditional religion, such as the trance states of the old shamans, and would perhaps have the prestige of being antinomian, marginal and slighty dangerous itself. Would this be a heady brew after a generation of tight social control which left little room for such manifestations? Yet it would be mistaken to regard this kind of faith as a serious threat to state power. In his detailed study of pentecostalism in the USA, Anderson concludes:

> "Pentecostalism has internalized in its adherents those characteristics and moral values that the society as a whole subscribes to, but only the lower are expected to live up to: passivity, obedience, honesty, hard work, thrift, self-denial and sobriety. In short, Pentecostalism has served the social function of developing the ideal proletariat for urban industrial capitalism – just as other sectarian movements have... Even the presumed 'radical' or 'extremist' practices of tongues, exorcism and healing are conservative in effect, because they have kept the Pentecostals busily engaged in activities which have no impact whatoever on the fundamental political economy or social relations of

51. Li, Yih-yuan, "Social Change, Religious Movements and Personality Adjustment: an Anthropological View", in D.Y.H. Yu, op. cit., p. 64.

American society, and because they serve to reconcile the Pentecostals to things as they are. Because these practices are so 'different' they have appeared to challenge the status quo, but they have been mere rituals of rebellion, cathartic mechanisms which in fact stabilize the social order[52]."

In a broader consideration of religions based on spirit possession, Lewis argues that they often become "religions of the oppressed" in moralistic, highly structured societies. They are in his view protest cults that enable the dispossessed - and especially women - "to advance their interests and improve their lot, even if only temporarily, from the confining bonds of their allotted station in society[53]". Lacking authentic mastery over their fate, the oppressed are attracted by ecstatic religion with its alternative reality. Anderson comes to a similar conclusion: "the radical social impulse inherent in the vision of the disinherited was transformed into social passivity, ecstatic escape, and finally a most conservative conformity[54]". We would suggest that such groups in China would prefer to stay out of the political arena altogether, and that only persecution would force them up to adopt clandestinity and perhaps political opposition.

Provisional Conclusions

Many questions need to be elucidated in depth as we work towards a greater understanding of religions in China. Until recently, Western research has tended to be dominated by issues of more immediate political impact: urban and rural development, foreign policy, party leadership. Chinese research on the other hand is primarily centred around the quest for modernization. Chinese intellectuals have a traditional disdain for peasant culture, the home of most religion, and many probably readily accede to state priorities which see religion as a minor nuisance rather than an important aspect of popular life. A common weakness of analysis of the PRC has been the obsessive focus on individual leaders, the implication that manipulations by a handful of senior individuals are sufficient to explain social processes in China. This view has many supporters. For media it provides explanations which are readily understood by consumers. For politicians it provides scapegoats and self-aggrandizement: for example the absurd characterization of the cultural revolution as essentially due to Jiang Qing's perversity.
Such analyses fail to explain complex, deep rooted social issues. Leaders are powerful to the extent that a population is powerless. An all powerful leader is in some sense a metaphor for a population that has very limited self-determina-

52. R.M. Anderson, *Vision of the Disinherited: the Making of American Pentecostalism*, New York: Oxford University Press, 1979, gives further reference to the role of pentecostalist and evangelist movements in industrializing societies, see particularly Chapter Twelve 'The Sources and Functions of Pentecostalism'.
53. Lewis, op. cit., p. 127.
54. Anderson, op. cit., p. 240.

tion, one that is fragmented, disinherited, unable to form a solid civil society despite frequent uprisings against particular regimes. Unfortunately throughout imperial times this was the actual condition of Chinese society according to most historians and scholars including communists. Basic elements in this situation were the fragmentation caused by local loyalties and rivalries, lack of a prosperous merchant and industrial class, and perhaps characteristics of the Chinese personality - tendencies to obedience and conformity - that have been theorized by Pye and others.

A profound change in the political situation can only take place if there is a profound change in fundamental structures of society and consciousness. Many structures have been shaken, if not overthrown, in the past forty years but there will need to be a further period of uncertainty about values, behaviour, morality and loyalty before China regains a period of deep stability and inner coherence. In the past western thought proposed various alternatives to the imperial system: democracy, fascism, socialism, technological efficiency, Christianity have all had their attractions and made a certain impact. But none of them has yet succeeded in fully 'winning the hearts and minds of the Chinese people' who live in a hybrid of Confucianism, Leninism and consumerism, in the throes of industrial development and social upheaval.

Because of the particular nature of communist ideology a dysfunction has arisen between the state and popular religious sentiment. Under the imperial regime there existed at least a congruence between élite, state religion and popular traditions: they were at different levels of sophistication but they inhabited the same universe. One was a reflection of the other. There were tensions between them but they could co-exist. Now, however, a great gulf appears to have opened between the religious, or quasi-religious, dimension of the state discussed earlier and the continuing deep hold of other religions. In a period when one could expect a flourishing of religious phenomena in Chinese society, the only fully legitimate expression of religious feeling is celebration of the state, while other forms are marginalized or even driven into illegality. This seems a short-sighted policy.

In the course of the paper we have discussed various working hypotheses. Most of them reflect the urgent need for fuller empirical data. To conclude this paper we list some of the more important areas for further investigation:

1. Data on Taoism, Buddhism and sectarianism are sadly lacking. Christianity fares a little better in this respect. State policy and the ideology of institutional religions are reasonably well documented but much needs to be done concerning the social functions of religion, popular beliefs and practices. Statistics concerning the numbers of believers vary enormously from different sources.

2. Religions in China will probably reflect the processes of social change there. The return to private farming in the 1980s may have contributed to the revival of religion in the countryside, and disillusion with the CCP may be an important factor in cities. Comparisons with other countries may be helpful in this respect.

3. Relations with the state, which range from accommodation to indifference and even opposition, form an important issue. The state itself has inherited a quaai-religious dimension and remains an intrusive element in the religious

field. Comparisons with church/state relations in other cultures may not be directly relevant.
4. The growth of evangelical Christianity may be related to the revival of sectarianism. There appear to be important areas of congruence between Christian and other sects. Both sectarianism and local traditions have survived vigorously into the 1990s and form an important element of popular life in some areas at least.

It is true that religious movements can blind adherents to social realities, but they can also be vehicles of social change and human dignity. Hundreds of millions of human beings in China are faced with the task of creating, something of profound meaning and value in their often difficult lives. Public disasters since 1949 have often led to personal tragedy, community trauma. In troubled times it is an essential human reaction to turn to questions of life and death, spirit and body, purity and corruption, serenity or mental illness. Perhaps some of these dramas are being enacted in the rituals of popular religion and the inner journeys of questioning intellectuals. This country with its tremendous religious heritage must integrate such aspirations towards meaningfulness.

~ context of quasi-relig. dimension of State well-being, & how it's failed.

2. A CHINESE PERSPECTIVE ON THE INTERPRETATION OF THE CHINESE GOVERNMENT'S RELIGIOUS POLICY

Kim-Kwong Chan

In the past decade, the international Christian communities have taken a special interest in the re-emergence of the Chinese Churches under the modernization policy promoted by the post-Mao Chinese Government. One of the important areas of interest has been the religious policy adopted by the Chinese Government after 1979. This policy was introduced in 1979, elaborated in a Central Party Document (no. 19) in 1982[1], affirmed in the constitution in 1983 and by 1988 was being formulated into a set of Religious Ordinances[2]. On the one hand, it permits a certain degree of freedom for believers to express their faith; on the other hand, it allows the government to exert strong control over religious affairs.

Within the context of communist ideology, adopted as state orthodoxy by the Chinese Government, this policy of limited religious freedom can be interpreted as a temporary measure to ensure that believers unite with the government in achieving the economic objectives of the nation, or as a means to limit the expansion of religion and safeguard the atheistic teaching of the State. A more extreme view would be to interpret it as a means of eliminating religion altogether, gradually achieving communism's ultimate goal of an atheistic utopia[3].

While these interpretations may be valid within the confined context of Communist ideology, it is possible to view the religious policy of the current government in the light of the Chinese historical experience and the control of religious affairs exercised by Chinese authorities since the Tang Dynasty. This paper will therefore suggest that the current religious policy in China is basically a continuation of the Chinese administrative tradition in religious affairs.

We begin with a brief survey of government administrative policies on religious affairs from the Tang Dynasty to the Qing Dynasty. We will examine some characteristics common to these policies, and compare them with features of current policy. It is hoped that, through this short study, it will be possible to establish a 'Chinese Perspective', seen from the point of view of Chinese rulers, on the polemics of religion in China. Furthermore, it is hoped that the discussion will serve as a catalyst to stimulate further research.

1. For a detailed treatment of this subject, see Kim-Kwong Chan, *Towards a Contextual Ecclesiology: The Catholic Church in the People's Republic of China (1979-1983); Its Life and Theological Implications*, Hong Kong: Phototech System Limited, 1987, Chapter One.
2. The Drafting Committees on Religious Ordinances of the Religious Affairs Bureau in Beijing circulated a mimeograph, dated April 1988, entitled: "Some Questions Concerning the Drafting of the Religious Ordinances".
3. Chan, op. cit., pp. 23-46.

Administration of Religious Affairs in the History of China

During the Tang Dynasty (618-907 CE), there were various government offices concerned with religious affairs. The most important one was the Office for the Worship of the Sombre Empyrean (*chongxuan shuling*), which came under the Board of Sacrifices (*cibu*). This office had a Director with the eighth rank and a Coadjutor with the ninth rank. Within it, there were two Archivists (*fu*), three Recorders (*shi*), six Overseers (*dianshi*), two Maintainers (*zhanggu*), one Doctor for the Study of the Worship of the Dark Universe (*chongxuanxue boshi*), and finally one hundred students or trainees. These officers kept records of Buddhist monks, including those foreigners, such as Japanese, who came to China to study Buddhism. Another office, the Director of Imperial Clan (*zongzheng*), was in charge of registration of Taoist priests[4].
These two offices, together with the Board of Sacrifices and the Department for Grades and Promotions (*sifeng*), controlled all religious affairs. Besides keeping records of clerics, they also imposed various restrictions. Monks could not lodge at a layman's place for more than three days, and clerics who traveled more than seven days had to apply for a special travel document from the local Prefect. A census of clerics was taken periodically. All licences for clerics were issued by the civil authorities. In some cases, as with the Edict issued by the Emperor Wuzong in 845, the government even laicized monks, demolished temples, and imposed restrictions on the total number of clerics.
Between the Tang and Song Dynasties (960-1280), the administration of religious affairs was undertaken by the Board of Sacrifices. This office examined candidates for tonsure and presided over all consecrations, imposing heavy penalties on those who carried out illegal consecrations. One can find documents recording the following:

> "And if anyone is consecrated surreptitiously, he and his Religious Instructors, together with the three Restrainers (*san gang zhishi*) who officiated at the altar, and the monks or nuns who were privy thereto, shall be punished. Whosoever is shaved surreptitiously, shall be compelled to go back to secular life, and his religious teacher shall be condemned to be beaten severely, and likewise be sent into exile for three years, with hard labour[5]."

It is interesting to note that the examination for tonsure candidates was held by the Board of Sacrifices and the content was set, not by a religious authority, but by government officials:

> "Boys over fifteen years of age, who can memorize by heart one hundred pages of sutras, or read five hundred pages of sutras; or girls over thirteen

4. Some of these historical data are based on J.J.M. de Groot *Sectarainaism and Religious Persecution in China*, 2 vols, Shannon: Irish University Press, 1974, which is a reprint of the 1903-04 edition The original sources have been checked and translation modified where necessary.
5. Ibid., p. 75.

years old, who can memorize seventy pages of sutras or read three hundred pages, can apply to the Prefect of the government for tonsure. This office will appoint an Official Secretary (*lushi*) or Archivist, and a judge, to examine them in their knowledge of the sutras[6]."

During the Song Dynasty, religious affairs were governed by the Office for the Registration of Buddhist Clerics (*seng lusi*) and the Office for the Registration for Taoist Priests (*dao lusi*). Both Offices were under the administration of the Board of Rites (*libu*), and they kept a tight control over the numbers and activities of the clerics. They also appointed Cleric Officers (*sengguan*), clerics who were government officials and supervised their clerical colleagues on behalf of the civil authority. Their contemporary equivalents would be the officials of the Three-Self Patriotic Movement of the Protestant Church and the Chinese Catholic Patriotic Association.

Song Emperors issued edicts imposing restrictions on religious activities, and one has to keep in mind that they were mainly Confucianists who despised religious believers. Emperor Renzong in 1033 prohibited any construction and restoration of temples, while an earlier imperial edict had even banned families from holding funeral services with Buddhist or Taoist rites[7]. The first Emperor of the Ming dynasty, although he had himself once been a monk, seemed to tighten rather than relax government control over religious affairs. The Registrar of the Buddhist and Taoist clergy was appointed, and police and garrison troops were entrusted to enforce edicts on religious affairs. For example, all clergy, friars and monasteries had to be correctly registered. The number of clerics and monasteries was determined according to the size of the administrative districts, causing many monasteries to close down and clerics to join government-sanctioned monasteries. Ordination certificates were issued once every three years by the government, and no person under the age of forty was allowed to become a monk or nun. New translations of Sacred Books were forbidden and no addition to the number of Sacred Books was tolerated. Religious ceremony and liturgy had to follow the directions of the civil authority.

Those who violated these decrees were subjected to severe punishment, which also extended to their families. They were imprisoned, made slaves, exiled to remote areas or handed over to the Board of Soldiers (*bingbu*) for conscript service in frontier regions[8]. All these decrees on religious affairs were codified in *The Fundamental And Supplementary Law To The Great Ming Dynasty*.

These Ming controls were maintained as the basic policy for religious administration under the Qing dynasty, and were further elaborated. Within the Offices of the Registrar for Buddhist and Taoist Clergy, the special posts of Expositor of the Religion (*chanjiao*) and Preacher of Scripture (*jiangjing*) were established to supervise Buddhists, and the Professor of Religion (*yanfa*) to oversee

6. Ibid., p. 73ff.
7. Ibid., p. 80.
8. Ibid., p. 84.

Taoists. Through these posts the government controlled religious activities, including the teaching of religion.

Furthermore, all monasteries and temples had to have official approval and, being the property of the government, were only temporarily entrusted to the clerics. Since all public locations for religious activities belonged to the government, many government agencies, such as the Board of Rites (*libu*), the Commandant of the Gendarmerie, the local Yamen (district offices cum police station), or the Court of Sacrificial Worship, could claim varying degrees of jurisdiction and authority over religious affairs. As under the Ming, all decrees on religious affairs were codified in law. For example, Chapter Eight, Article Three of *The Fundamental and Supplementary Law of the Great Qing Dynasty* entitled: "On Private Founding of Monastic Building and Private Ordination of Buddhist and Taoist Monks," specified that those who violated the decree would receive one hundred blows with the long stick; monks would be laicized and banished forever to the furthest frontier of the Empire; nuns would be appropriated by the government as slaves; and properties would be confiscated.

There were also laws to restrict the admission of neophytes. Only families with at least three sons could offer a boy to be a monk, and all neophytes had to be without a criminal record. Anyone breaking these laws would be laicized and severely punished, and any cleric involved with such crimes would lose his state-issued consecration licence and would himself be laicized.

The Current Situation

From this brief historical survey, one can detect attitudes towards religious administration that were common to the Chinese civil authorities in different periods. The secular authorities always assumed the right to control religious affairs. Although religious workers (clerics) had a low social status, the government did not underestimate their potential influence and sought to reinforce its control by various administrative methods, including military force. The use of such extreme measures by the government suggests that it was liable to regard religion as a security, rather than an ideological, issue, especially at times when religious groups had gained significant economic and political power. For example, Wuzong of the Tang Dynasty had to curb the social influence of Buddhists by the enforced laicization of one quarter of a million monks and nuns and the confiscation of millions of acres of land belonging to the monasteries. In a population of sixty to seventy million, to have one quarter of a million adults (monks and nuns) paying no taxes and exempt from military draft, invited a drastic response from the Emperor.

The degree of religious freedom, then, was determined by the government, and Chinese rulers assumed that they had the absolute authority – through the Mandate of Heaven – to control the lives of their people, including their religious beliefs and practices[9]. They believed that they exercised this authority for the

9. The concept of the Mandate of Heaven in the minds of Chinese rulers is discussed in Chapter Six

welfare of the nation, not for the liberty of the individual. For example, the government officially endorsed many religious practices, such as ancestor worship, and officially promoted certain deities, like Chenhuang and Tianhou in Southern China. It was evident that these officially-sanctioned practices either posed no political threat to the government or were under its direct control. Religious movements outside official control, such as the White Lotus Sect or the Nian uprising in the Qing Dynasty, could not be tolerated by a government that regarded them as a threat to the welfare of Chinese society.

There is a striking similarity between the administration of religious affairs by the present Chinese Government and that of its dynastic predecessors. It openly exercises its authority over the Chinese people, and this attitude is reflected in the Document no. 19 of 1982, which indicates that it is the professed duty of the ruling authority, the Chinese Communist Party, to regulate religious affairs[10]. Members of the Party, not Chinese religious believers, have the responsibility to formulate policy towards religion in the post-Mao society. This policy includes civil control over the location of religious activities, the teaching of doctrine, ceremony (liturgy), the education of laity, the training of clerical candidates, the appointment of high ranking clerics, relations with overseas religious groups, the propagation of faith, and the production of religious materials. Further examples of this can be found in the Communist Party Central Document no. 3 issued in 1989 concerning the increase of government control over the Catholic Church[11].

All these facets of religious affairs, normally understood by Western Christians, especially Protestants, as being in the religious domain and matters to be decided by believers under the principle of religious freedom, are determined by the Chinese government with an authority reminiscent of the Mandate of Heaven. This approach to religious administration seems to be a continuation of a Chinese administrative tradition that can be traced back to the Tang Dynasty. If one compares the present with the past, at the juridical level, believers may seem to enjoy more freedom now than in the past. However, the extent of religious freedom in practice very much depends on the attitude of the local authorities. As a result, official treatment of religion can be very oppressive in one region, and more liberal elsewhere. Also, penalties imposed on those who violated religious decrees in the past seem to have been more severe than those applied by the present government, but since 1949 believers in China have often been sen-

of C.K. Yang's *Religion in Chinese Society*, Berkeley: University of California Press, 1961. There are similarities to be found in the notion of the subordination of ecclesiastical to civil authority in the tradition of the Orthodox Church; it was also shared by the western church in medieval times.

10. *Zhonggong zhongyang wenjian 19 hao: (guanyu woguo shehuizhuyi shiqi zongjiao wenti di jiben zhengce) di tongzhi* (CCP Central Committee Document no. 19: Circular (Concerning China's Basic Standpoint and Policy on Religious Questions in the Socialist Period)). Beijing: CCP Central Committee Confidential Document, 31 March 1982. An English translation can be found in McInnis, Donald E., *Religion in China Today: Policy and Practice*, Maryknoll: Orbis Books, 1989.

11. For a summary of this document see *Zhongguo yu jiaohui* (China and the Chuch Today) no 77, May-June 1990, pp. 11-12.

tenced to long prison terms for the political crimes of being anti-revolutionary or reactionary elements, and not for directly violating decrees on religion.

From this preliminary study, we can conclude that government control over religious affairs has a long tradition in China, and is deeply rooted in the minds of the ruling class. While the present religious policy of the Chinese Communist Party, the de facto government of China, may reasonably be interpreted as the result of the anti-religious nature of Communist ideology, it may also be viewed as a continuation of traditional government practices intensified by Communist anti-religious sentiment. It thus derives from the historical experience of the exercise of imperial power by the country's rulers. More detailed research may reveal further continuities, but available evidence already suggests that the "Chinese Perspective" is a fruitful approach to understanding the whole polemic on religion, especially Christianity, in China.

From this "Chinese Perspective", the China-Vatican relationship can be viewed as a conflict of two cultures over the issue of Church and State. Unless the understanding of Heavenly Mandate changes, one can hardly imagine the Chinese government allowing its subjects to form a community, or church with allegiance to a foreign political entity, the Vatican. On the other hand, if Rome insists on its administrative authority over Catholics in China, as with its policy of Ostpolitik towards Eastern Bloc Catholic Churches, and disregards the unique cultural tradition of the Chinese civil administration, it may find very little common ground for dialogue with the Chinese government in its search for reunion with the Catholic Church in China.

There are a few other elements which also affect the thinking of the current Chinese rulers concerning religious control. A xenophobic mentality and anti-foreign sentiment, resulting from the past national humiliations China suffered, may have influenced the Chinese leaders to impose a tighter control over the activities of imported religions, such as Christianity. The international dimension of commerce and trade may force China to open its doors to foreign culture. However, one should not be too optimistic about international influences having an immediate bearing on the possible loosening of religious control by the Chinese authorities. The Cultural Revolution and more recently the negative response by the Chinese government to democratization in the Eastern Bloc suggests that Chinese leaders, in the short term at least, will opt for ideological purity rather than economic prosperity.

Some questions in the areas of Chinese Studies and theology emerge from this discussion: 1) What is the relationship between Communist ideology and the concept of the Mandate of Heaven in the minds of the current Chinese leadership vis-a-vis religious policy? 2) When Chinese authorities insist on strong control over religious affairs, what are the connections between their various motives: to safeguard state orthodoxy; to consolidate the ruling authority; or to assume the traditional duty of the Mandate of Heaven? 3) What is the role of the 'cleric officers' of today (i.e. officials in the 'patriotic' religious organisations) in the context of the Chinese civil administration, and in the context of the ecclesiastical communities? 4) How does the foreign nature of Christianity influence the minds of Chinese leadership in formulating religious policy? 5) In the context of the Chinese civil administration of religious affairs, what are the theological ramifications of ecclesiology? 6) What is the meaning of faith in the victorious power of the Resurrected Christ for a powerless ecclesiastical community living under the rule of a secular authority? 7) And finally, perhaps the most crucial question: what will be the fate of Christianity in a state where the traditional concept of the Mandate of Heaven is deeply embedded in the minds of the rulers?

"registration" a key pt,
continuity well argued

3. THE OLD AND THE NEW: A COMMENTARY ON THE CONTROL OF POPULAR RELIGION IN THE PRC

Stephan Feuchtwang

The invention of tradition is by now a well-researched theme in the study of the cultures of nations[1]. Monuments, postage stamps, and currency celebrate the moments of foundation, the famous defences and the claims to fame of nations. They constitute an official memory, a patriotic history inscribed in school curricula. Personally traced and officially installed, it is at once new and claims to be ancient, the finding and renewal of a primordial nature. The composition of this identity also includes the anthems, the emblems, the ceremonials and the official calendar of commemorating a nation, in short, a political or a civil religion. Commemoration and celebration of a people's identity are in addition sometimes endorsed by a denomination of a universal religion - such as the Anglican church of Christianity. But in so doing, religion becomes complicit in what is a local and an historical project of the formation of a state and a people.

Recent studies have gone further, to grapple with the ambivalences involved in the semi-conscious construction of tradition. They focus on the necessary processes of forgetting discrepancies and selectively remembering what is appropriate to the present of the people. They show how appeals to a people differentiated from others also contain defensive mechanisms, by which the others are characterized with the attributes which are repressed or are indefensible in the common senses of popular national identification and its ideologies[2].

Republics led by Communist parties have been no exception to this ambivalence, which is also a paradox and a pathology, of nation-building. The paradox and pathology are, if anything, more acute for Communist republics. Their investment in the construction of traditions is more centrally administered and more populist[3]. First, the appeal to a people is all the more urgent for the claim of Communist parties to represent the masses. This is a people which, common to all nationalist claims, has 'always' been there. But, second, the construction and the writing of a history-tradition is, even more than for the USA and France, a universal as well as a local truth. It is a truth not only of human development but of revolution.

For all nations, history is the tracing of an aspiration and a project - which is the fulfilling of the potential of a people and the achievement of prosperity, fre-

1. Eric Hobshawm and Terence Ranger (eds), *The Invention of Tradition*, Cambridge University Press, 1983.
2. See for example Benedict Anderson, *Imagined Communities*, London: Verso, 1983, and the even more acute work of Homi Bhabha (ed), *Nation and Narration*, London: Routledge, 1990.
3. For the construction of a civic religion in the Soviet Union, see Christel Lane, *The Rites of Rulers; Ritual in an Industrial Society - the Soviet Case*, Cambridge University Press, 1981.

quently recounted in schemata of modernization or of development, the successors to nineteenth-century doctrines of progress. But revolution is rupture, a qualitative leap into a new state of social relations and of cultural conditions corresponding to it. This was true for the dissidents who settled in the new world and eventually threw off their colonial ties and masters. It was also peculiarly true of the country which prides itself as the epitome of humanist enlightenment and its revolution. But for both the USA and France this was once and for all. For Communists the revolution is a continuing process – their traditions are future-oriented to a peculiarly emphatic degree. The construction of the socialist nation is never complete. There will be, and are intended to be, future ruptures. And if there is a moment of completion, it will be the dissolution of nations and their states in the international association of a global Communism. Yet their representation of the masses must root each Communist party and its masses in a nation. They each rule, as do the rulers of other nations, in the name of a 'people', which is inscribed in the role of being the subject of a long and continuous, if revolutionary, history. The maintenance of that subject's unity, the protection of its home territory are the tasks of Communist as they are of all other nation-states.

The paradox of a new tradition is greatest of all for the culture which claims the longest continuous history in the world. China's new historical tradition is that of popular uprising, of a peasantry despised or forgotten in the historiography of the imperial dynasties, a history of the common people in their long struggle for eventual mastery under the leadership of the Communist party. After each political crisis, the Chinese Communist Party inscribes a turning in that history from a reverse or a defeat. It reconstructs its history, its constitutions and its calendar of commemorations: its political religion.

It is in this context that we are bound to view the conduct in China of religious activities, whether they be of the named universal religions, or of that much more widespread and amorphous range of activities with which I shall be concerned: popular religion. The ambivalence of backward masses being raised to modern nationhood, of the revolutionary class of peasantry to be transformed into a modern class of socialist producers, and in particular the ambivalence of the task of transforming superstitions which are also the traditions of the Chinese nation will be my subject.

(PRC)

Imperial Cults And Republican Festivals

In another part of this volume, Kim-Kwong Chan has traced the history of imperial Chinese control of religious activities, and he does this in order to persuade us of the similarity, indeed the continuity, of the current People's Republican policy of control with its imperial predecessors. When we note that the imperial regime had official cults, including the emperor's prerogative to worship heaven and his own ancestors with the mandate of heaven, it is tempting to see in them a continuity with the civic religion of the republican state calendar, even though its occasions are quite different: Nation Day, Party Day, Workers

Day, Women's Day, Youth Day, Children's Day, etc. Kim-Kwong Chan stresses the continuity of Chineseness. I would rather stress the similarity of China with other nation-constructions, and therefore the distinctiveness of the republican from the imperial regime and its control of religious activities. If there is any continuity, it is greatest, not in the republican regime's civil religion, but in the popular festivals, some of which it endorses to control and others which it denounces to eliminate.

Gradually in the 1950s all but one of the former popular festivals were removed from official recognition. The one which remained in official recognition was and is that of the lunar new year, renamed Spring Festival. But it was and is the national festival to which the longest statutory holiday is attached. In the 1980s, a number of others were restored to recognition in publications of the official calendar, including *qingming* (Clear and Bright), *duanwu* (the Double Fifth), the Autumn Festival, and the Winter Solstice.

Two state organizations in the People's Republic have prime responsibility for governing religious activities. One is the system of bureaux of Religious Affairs, which is an agency directly responsible to the State Council. The other is the system of Culture bureaux, which is part of the Ministry of Culture. The system of Religious Affairs bureaux is principally one of regulation through registration. Any organization of religious activity which wants, within the confines of the constitutional right to religious freedom, to proceed openly in public must be registered. This is certainly a bureaucracy similar to that of the imperial regime, even though the imperial bureaux and their registers of religious organizations were authorized by an office of teaching and correction rather than by republican concepts of right, responsibility and freedom. The substantial difference between the two appears when we turn to the work of the system of Culture bureaux.

Culture Bureaux and Popular Festivals

The system of Culture Bureaux promulgates and promotes the official festivals of the Republican calendar and seeks to transform into what are considered healthy, the backward or malign tendencies of popular religious practices. Again, it must be noted that the imperial regime, through its own official cults at county level and above, and the adoption into them of some of the most popular cults, as well as through a system of surveillance and didactic rewards and punishments in rolls of honour and of shame at sub-county levels, had for long played just such a transformative role[4]. But this is merely to note the fact

4. On the adoption of popular cults into the official cults of the imperial regime, see Stephan Feuchtwang, "School Temple and City God", in Arthur P. Wolf (ed.), *Studies in Chinese Society*, Stanford University Press, 1978 and James Watson, "Standardising the Gods: The Promotion of T'ien Hou ('Empress of Heaven') Along the South China Coast, 960-1960" in David Johnson, Andrew J. Nathan and Evelyn S. Rawski (eds), *Popular Culture in Late Imperial China*, Berkeley: University of California Press, 1985. On the sub-county system of surveillance, see Michael Dutton, "Policing the Chinese Household: A Comparison of Modern and

that there was and is a system of transformative intervention. The new official calendar of festivals seeks to unite the common people into an integrated national sense of a shared revolutionary history. It promulgates a common Chineseness which has led to a common integrated present day of modernization.

While the republican festivals seek to include all sections of the population, the imperial state cults were exclusive. The imperial cults of the cosmic elements (Thunder, Rain, Mountains, Rivers, etc.) and of the Sages (Confucius, Mencius, Guan Gong) filtered out the uneducated while inducing in them a respect for a small educated élite to which they could aspire and in the meantime must defer. Even in his use of the cult of the City God, which he shared with the general populations of the administrative area, the educated administrator was the agent of an emperor who mediated between heaven and earth to maintain harmonious order, which the uneducated might otherwise endanger.

Some of this didacticism is present in the task of ideological work to which the Culture bureaux are assigned. But mass participation in official festivals is new, just as the maintenance of mass schooling and mass literacy is new and republican. The task of the Culture bureaux, pursued in a wide range of activities, is that of raising 'mass culture' (which is the name of their journal) to what is perceived as progressive levels. Popular religion is accordingly described as 'superstition', where it does not fit either the concept of universal and organized religion or the more neutral and national-historical concept of custom. Both superstition and religion are considered backward, but superstition is a remnant and a hindrance while religion is still helpful in the primary stage of socialism, which is where Chinese development has reached according to the current, post-1978, leadership. According to this explanation, 'superstition' persists because of low levels of spiritual civilisation. Religion, on the other hand, can inspire a sense of moral discipline and social obligation compatible with socialism.

Custom is part of Chinese history, continuity and tradition. It can be patriotic and can serve similar purposes of preserving a sense of obligation which religion can. But like religion, it is difficult to distinguish from superstition. What was in a previous line condemned as superstition can now be preserved as custom. For example, in pre-1978 periods ancestral worship during the Clear and Bright Festival (*qingmingjie*) was considered to be against socialism. It was condemned as a superstitious practice. The policy aim was to replace this practice with visits to tombs and memorials for revolutionary martyrs. But since 1978, ancestor worship has been recognized as a good custom which may contribute to China's modernization, as it helps to emphasize reliance on family support for social security and welfare, and it attracts visits by overseas Chinese to their homes and inspires them to invest in the motherland. So while schools and some work units organize visits to the monuments for revolutionary heroes which exist in every town and city, in villages, particularly of the two southeastern provinces

Ancient Forms", in *Economy and Society*, vol 17 no 2, May 1988. For the official cult of the City God, to which I refer a few lines further on, see David Johnson, "The City God Cults of T'ang and Sung China", *Harvard Journal of Asiatic Studies* no 45, 1985 and A.R. Zito, "City Gods, Filiality, and Hegemony in Late Imperial China", *Modern China*, vol 13 no 3, 1987.

(Fujian and Guangdong) from which the ancestors of most overseas Chinese emigrated, incense is burned and offerings are placed in front of domestic altars, feasts are held, and graves are cleaned and flagged with new paper spirit-emblems without fear of reprisals.

In other regions, or at other occasions, the Culture bureaux may still condemn such practices and the local Party will paste up exhortations to cease, backed-up by Public Security bureau condemnations of waste and social disturbance. In one village of Fujian which I visited in 1988, where the *qingming* 'custom' was tolerated, propitiation of orphan souls in the autumn General Salvation Festival (*pudu*) was condemned in these terms as 'superstition'.

Waste and disturbance were the very terms of imperial elite condemnation of popular religious feasting and festival. But now they are ambivalently condemned as the backward elements of the very people who are the makers of Chinese history. China's nation- and republic-building bears with any other this ambivalence towards the pre-industrial population, usually referred to as 'peasants' with all the derogatory implications this has of rural idiocy, while at the same time locating in them the idyllic root of national identity. In the case of China this ambivalence affects all persuasions in the creation of works of art or political commentary, as well as those expressed in the official tasks of ideological work and education.

Take for instance a short story published in 1981 and written by Dai Qing, a woman who became famous for her critical journalism. (She was jailed in the aftermath of spring 1989, and released in May 1990 without having been charged). It is a story entitled "No"[5], a reflection on his life by Commissar Liu at the end of a successful career of Party loyalty. His second wife tends him in ailing old age, nurturing a figure of conformity and high status, but her deliberate, soft-spoken tones begin to stifle him like a light bed of eiderdown. He begins to long for the hard bed of village life. He remembers his first wife, left in the village home, and the death of his father "on the kang (brick bedstand) that had served him as a bed all his life". The father is viewed from the familiar Chinese perspective of the village as ancestral home, but now also as the origin and simple basis of the revolution. "Ah, how much better to be like his father – sleeping peacefully on the foothills, bathed in sunshine and wild flowers, the spot marked by a solidly erected stone tablet coarsely inscribed: 'Communist Party member Liu Dayong'."

Thus Commissar Liu, wistful about the virtue of simple Party member Liu, left behind in his father's grave. To the villagers, on the other hand, "Liu was a high-ranking official of the Party, a well-intentioned man whom they knew well. They had watched him grow up." The reverse perspective of revolutionary nostalgia is patronage. The villagers can find the neighbour-of-origin path through bureaucracy to leap levels to a protector who can bring down his authority upon lower levels which had blocked or been deaf to villagers' grievances. The appeal in the story is to the Communist good intention of being

5. Its English translation was published in the *Bulletin of Concerned Asian Scholars*, vol 16 no 3, 1983.

in touch with the masses, not to nepotism. But it is ambiguous at best, and once more there is a striking similarity with the imperial regime, in this case to reliance on petition (ultimately to the emperor), for the righting of wrongs. But here it is a petition to the party of the people, not the emperor of heaven and earth.

The Construction of Republican Progress

A republic is, in the course of construction, discarding some and preserving other elements of a pre-republican order and the popular religious practices that grew under it. In preserving, it transforms. What it cannot use it tries to relegate into a past as if to forget what is incompatible with the new historical narrative. The materials of this narrative are at various removes from current leaderships and their lines of applying the principles of a Communist republic. Above all, however, that leadership is national, not imperial. It must pay nominal and formal respect to the constituency which it seeks to represent and to lead, 'the people' whose integrated sovereign mass it is bringing into being in the processes of political education, scientific schooling and economic advance. Even if official and commoner (the hundred names) are still part of the cast, they are removed from the vocabulary and the narrative of past sages and the four Confucian classes of scholar, farmer, artisan and merchant in the eternal order of heaven and earth. They have been transformed into the acutely ambivalent relationship between the people and its leaders.

The mixture of revolutionary with ancestral origin, Party with imperial authority, is characteristic of the political culture of the modernizing republic of China. Its historical burden is exceptional only in the long duration of imperial rule, apparently unchanged despite waves of massive peasant rebellion toppling dynasty after dynasty. Despite appearances, the system of rule, of property, and of bondage did, of course, change and so did the nature and the relations of economic production and exchange. Now the appearances themselves, the forms both of history and of political rule have changed. Imperial historiography was one of the restoration of order. It has changed into the nationalist form of history. It is now a narrative of modernization.

This is true whether it is official history and its celebratory calendar, or fictive biography like "No", or another critical history, like the film "Yellow Earth", directed by Chen Kaige (1984). Here 'superstitious' rain-making rituals, made to look more like the stereotype of tribal magic, end a story of Party failure even in its revolutionary spring to transform peasant culture from within. At the same time the rituals stand for what critical political commentators have called 'modern superstition', referring to the adulation of Mao or of Deng Xiaoping as the new emperor. The political passivity of the peasantry, punctuated by eruptions of egalitarian wrath and the search for a new leader, is seen as the heritage of a backward and unscientific, antidemocratic, way of life. And the old men in charge are criticized as peasant-minded strategists in search of their own immortality in the historical record.

For their part, officially sanctioned studies and histories of Chinese rural customs and religion attempt a separation of the true from the false in, for instance, the stories attached to local deities. They also attempt to discern and separate the healthy and useful from the wasteful and the disturbing in the practices of divination, petition, and thanksgiving which local festivals entail. In these studies, the narrative of modernization condemns to wasteful and disturbing backwardness, what another official narrative seeks to record and preserve as an element of Chinese culture, its true origins and its continuity as the heritage of the common people[6].

Researchers from the Culture bureaux investigated the resurgence of 'feudal superstitious activities' as they called them in rural north China. Extracts, which follow, from the beginning, middle and end of the report of their research should give an idea of the framing narrative of modernization in which their work as well as their reports are couched[7]. Superstition is the word for what is decried because it refuses to recede into the past.

> "Nowadays, it is of great benefit to develop research broadly on village mass culture, its good and its bad aspects, and start exploring differences in the furtherance of the twofold (material and spiritual) construction of socialist civilization and the spreading of unblemished people's culture.
>
> For this reason, in June-July 1987 we embarked on sample investigations of the conditions of feudal superstitious activities in different economic, cultural, and geographic situations in the Han Zhong region of Shaanxi province.
>
> *The general situation of rural feudal superstitious activities*
>
> It was with the profoundest sorrow that we were brought to acknowledge that, more than thirty years after the construction of the PRC and despite the overthrow of the feudal system, feudal superstitious activities still prevail.
>
> [...]
>
> In a village in Chadianzhen, Mianxian, when in 1986 a village-wide movement to restore a temple emerged, all the cadres and eleven Party members took part. [...One of them] took part in [the procession ritual of] 'sending out spirits to see off demons' [...]
>
> There are feudal superstitious activists in the plains, in the mountains, in prosperous and in poor places. According to our investigation in Baolianqu,

6. On officially sanctioned studies and histories of traditional customs and popular religion see Stephan Feuchtwang, "The Problem of "Superstition" in the People's Republic of China", in G. Benavides (ed.), *Religion and Political Power*, Albany: State University of New York Press, 1989 and Stephan Feuchtwang and Wang Mingming, "The Politics of Culture or a Contest of Histories: Representations of Chinese Popular Religion", *Dialectical Anthropology*, (forthcoming).
7. Zhou Ying, "Fengjian mixin yu qunzhong wenhua; guanyu Han Zhong fengjian mixin huodong de diaocha yu yanjiu" ("Feudal Superstition and Mass Culture; On the Investigation and Research into Feudal Superstitious Activities in Han Zhong"), in *Qunzhong Wenhua* (Mass Culture), No 5, 1988. I am most grateful to Wang Mingming, not only for drawing my attention to this article but also for much information concerning the changes in officially recognised festivals.

> Mianxian, (a plains area), there were 135 witches and sorcerers engaged in superstitious activities, of whom 9 had emerged in the 1950s, 23 in the 1960s and 1970s, but 103 in the 1980s. In the past, most would have been old men and women, but in recent years not a few entering such activities have been middle-aged and young. [...]
> - where feudal superstition is rampant, where is the spiritual support to accompany agrarian modernization? Can it depend on 'demon souls' and 'spirit powers'?
> - for those who place their hopes on material things, where is their 'spiritual garden'? Can feudal superstition calm their hearts and raise their spirits?
> - among the young who return to the country upon graduation are some in the course of wandering high in the mountains and deep in the forests seeking a spiritual life, and where should they look? Back to feudal superstition?"

Contrast that modernizing condemnation with another report, this time by academics, but written as usual with policy recommendations in mind. This one is in the preservative mode, in which the Ministry of Culture as well as academics investigate the cultural productions of localities and place them in historical context, in which artifacts and documents are preserved in museums, buildings are refurbished for internal and foreign tourism, and practitioners are encouraged to record and continue their arts. It is a report on rural musicians in another part of north China, Hebei province.
After strictly musical considerations of what the musicians in the village remember and play now, the article traces the foundation of the village and how it became a centre of local musical art. It then describes what it calls the 'uses' of the music. But it does this without recourse to explanations, so makes no references to economic and cultural conditions in human evolution:

> "In the old times, Qu Jia Ying's important occasions for the performance of orthodox-style music were of five kinds."

These are, as sub-titled, 1. lunar new year temple tour; 2. going to fairs to pay obeisance at temples; 3. seeking rain in droughts; 4. commemorating the Master of Vastness (a local deity) and entertaining spirits generally (at the seventh month festival of ghosts); 5. funerals. I will cite just the first:

> "In the past there were seven large and small temples in the village, in which were enshrined deities, most of which came from the *Enfeoffment of the Spirits*, the *Journey to the West*, and other Ming and Qing dynasty stories and records of strange things. They included a Military Spirit Temple, Three Passes Temple, a Temple to the King of Purgatory, a Dragon God Temple, a Reclining Goddess of Mercy Temple, and others. The most important use of these temples was for villagers' prayers to avert calamity and bring good fortune; if in any family someone wanted, they could go to the temple, select a deity and pay obeisance, burn incense and make a pledge. Since normally there were no ceremonies of collective offerings, on the first day of the first

month each year the Music Association represented the wishes of the whole village by touring and performing for the pleasure of the deities of each temple, praying for good fortune and to redeem pledges, and this was called 'touring the temples'[8]."

The temples, the deities, the prayers to them and their annual joint festival procession are thus described as matters of local and of more general historical interest. The more general interest is in the sources to which the legends of the deities can be traced, in the texts of popular stories and dramas. The local interest is in the choice of deities and the way their festival was performed distinctively from the festivals of another speciality: the Music Association. The temples no longer exist, but a new-year ceremonial organized around village Music Associations, without a tour of temples, takes place now in several villages visited by folklorist investigators in Hebei. In this mode of investigation, music and festival are given an academic historical pedigree which corrects some of the claims to originality made by the musicians and villagers, but they are not condemned as a backward and socially disturbing relic.

Condemnation jostles preservation. Culture bureaux try to do both by separating the progressive and historically authentic from the backward and disturbing. But often the task is impossible and contradictory. The revivals, the remembered and preserved rites and practices are mixed with inventions and adaptations - often through the medium of spirit possession or spirit writing - responding to current economic and political uncertainties. They are both historical and contemporary, preserved and disturbing. In particular, they fill a space left by the evacuation of village Party leadership, translated into entrepreneurial activities. Old and new deities are celebrated, old and new ways of resolving uncertainties through divination are practised. Objects of petition for securing good outcomes to dicey decisions, guardians against demonic breakdowns of health or fortune, the deities are the heroes of a locally reinvented and sanctified history, always taken from the imperial era. Often they are martyrs, who died in defence of comrades or of the common people or in dedication to saving people from the vagaries of travel or disease, or from purgatorial and imperial wrath. Their festivals, new temples, and the pledges and questions addressed to them are forms of local identification, a local sense of history and continuity. Alongside it, within and across the boundaries and intervals it marks, new kinds of self-organization grow. They are largely economic, not political, and they participate, through marketing, migration and through the reception of radio and other mass media, with the more urban routines and calendars governed by the official republic.

Meanwhile, in the cities, official occasions and the martyrs they too celebrate are kept. Shadowing them are alternative heroes and dates. The prospects of

8. Xue Yibing and Wu Ben, "Qu Jia Ying 'yinyuehui' de diaocha yu yanjiu" ("Investigations and Research into the 'Music Association' of Qu Jia Ying"), *Zhongguo Yinyuexue* (Musicology in China), 1987, p. 89. Warmest thanks to Steven Jones, musician and musicologist, for supplying me with a copy of this article.

further change, of re-minding and re-fixing the ceremonials of republics and their histories, have been dramatically opened by the upheavals of Chinese and European socialist republics in 1989. But whatever they might be, they too will have an uneasy relationship to the rural histories and identifications which they would prefer to either forget or to turn into a heritage.

Urban entertainment, schools, and the news media, are now as never before points of reference for the rural population. If rural histories and customs find any reflection in them, it is likely to be a denying one, patronizing of rural backwardness or envious of wasted, ostentatious rural wealth including that spent on feast and festival. But the denial and reactions to it are part of the dynamic process in which a Chinese political culture is being created and contested.

— blah. Not useful for review.

4. SOME REFLECTIONS ON PROTESTANT LIFE IN CHINA

Bob Whyte

The purpose of this paper is to discuss some key issues relating to the current situation of the Protestant Church in China. It is not intended to offer a detailed description of the day to day life of the Church as there are many accounts of church life in China, all of which witness to its vitality[1]. The experiences of persecution, especially in the ten long years of the Cultural Revolution from 1966 to 1976, have resulted in a depth of faith which is obvious to even a casual visitor. Yet, serious problems are facing Chinese Christians and these are growing more urgent as time goes on.

It is proposed to look first at the long standing issue of the relationship of Christianity to Chinese culture. This kind of question faces believers in all societies, but it is particularly acute in China, for Chinese culture has until now shown itself to be remarkably impervious to the Christian message.

The next major issue to be discussed is the question of the unity of the Church. Historically, Protestant Christians in China have shown themselves to be reluctant to consider ecclesiological issues. Today, as far as the internal life of the Church is concerned, this is the key question. What does it mean to be a part of the 'one, holy, catholic and apostolic Church'? Or is the principle of catholicity redundant? At stake is the very understanding of the Church and therefore of the relationship of Christians one to another, and to Christ Himself.

The last major issue to be considered is the actual organization of Church life. This immediately raises the issue of the relationship between Church and State specifically focussing on the nature of the China Christian Council and its relationship to the Three Self Patriotic Movement (TSPM).

Finally, there are some important subsidiary issues which relate to these three major areas in one way or another which will be briefly discussed.

Christianity and Chinese Culture

Historical Retrospect

Traditional Chinese culture has been moulded by Confucianism with its this worldly and ethical emphasis. Philosophical Taoism has certainly provided a counterpoint to the main theme, usually expressed within art and poetry and often representing the private face of the official who in public life was Confu-

1. See for example issues of *Bridge* magazine published by the Christian Study Centre on Chinese Religion and Culture, Hong Kong.

cian. Buddhism had its greatest impact in the centuries before the great persecution of 845, and while it has continued as a significant aspect of Chinese culture, its most creative contribution was made in the early centuries after its introduction to China. From the Song dynasty onwards Neo-Confucianism dominated public life, having developed its own metaphysics in response to the Buddhist challenge. When the Jesuit missionaries, led by Matteo Ricci, arrived in China in the late 16th century as the Ming dynasty was moving to its close, the dominant intellectual force in society was Confucian. It was not, therefore, surprising that the Jesuits focused their attention on Confucianism. Moreover, it was the Confucian literati who expressed interest in the ideas of the Western religion and who befriended Ricci. The Jesuits had little time for Buddhism or Taoism for in the late Ming religious Taoism had merged into popular religion and, to the outsider, Buddhism appeared little different from popular superstition[2].

In the 19th century when Catholic missionaries returned to China and the Protestants arrived for the first time, Chinese culture was in serious decline. Conservative Christianity, whether Catholic or Protestant, was the major force within Christian missions to China in the 19th century and the attitudes of the missionaries were very different from those of the early Jesuits. Ricci and his confrères appreciated Confucian culture as an expression of the human spirit worthy of respect. Their 19th century successors came with a view of human culture as necessarily in conflict with the Gospel and therefore they did not encourage an encounter with Chinese culture, rather, they sought to 'rescue' their converts from the darkness of 'heathenism' and unbelief. The churches they founded saw themselves over against a hostile pagan world. The objective situation in which they found themselves reinforced this attitude, for Christianity had only survived in China after the Kangxi Emperor issued his Edict of 1721, banning the Christian religion, by going underground. The Catholic policy of creating Catholic villages, enclaves amidst a pagan world, was an obvious response to persecution, but it was also rooted in theological hostility to 'paganism' by foreign missionaries. Protestants, sharing a similar hostile view of paganism, nevertheless adopted a different policy in which medical, educational and welfare work played a significant role for they also believed that their mission included bringing the benefits of modern European civilization to China[3].

The winds of liberalism began to blow through the Protestant churches in the West in the later 19th century and by the 1920s led in China to a division between fundamentalist missionaries and 'liberals' who espoused the 'social gospel'. In the 1920s attempts were made by a small number of Protestant theologians to look at the relationship between Christianity and Confucianism, but by this time Confucianism was no longer seen as a viable philosophy by Chinese

2. For the attitude of the Jesuits to Confucianism and Buddhism see: Jacques Gernet, *China and the Christian Impact*, Cambridge University Press, 1985; and Jonathan D. Spence, *The Memory Palace of Matteo Ricci*, London: Faber, 1984.
3. See Bob Whyte, *Unfinished Encounter*, London: Collins Fount, 1988, especially Chapter 3, "To Save Souls, 1721-1860".

intellectuals and the attempt was soon abandoned. Alone amongst Chinese theologians T.C. Chao (Zhao Zichen) took matters further in the direction of getting to grips with what is distinctive in the Chinese spirit in his study of the poetry of Tao Yuanming. He realized that it was not enough to look at the official Confucian culture, and he perceived that it was Taoism that perhaps provided the key link in a meaningful dialogue. His attempt foundered on the rocks of war and revolution, but it stands today as a pointer towards new possibilities[4]. Catholic Modernism led to similar divisions within the Roman Catholic Church in the West but it hardly touched Catholic missionaries in China nor Chinese Catholics.

This all too brief survey points to an important fact. Christianity in China in 1949 remained deeply influenced by European theological and cultural presuppositions. We may qualify this statement by noting that on the level of popular faith the ethos of Chinese Christian life was profoundly, if unconsciously, influenced by the surrounding culture. So, for example, the Confucian view of the importance of morality within the 'good' life certainly led many in the late 19th and early 20th centuries to espouse Christianity as a moral philosophy. However, after the First World War Marxism was able to claim to provide a superior moral 'Way' and there were many defections from the Church by intellectuals, initially sympathetic towards Christianity, to the Communist Party from the 1920s until after 'Liberation' in 1949.

The Response to Communism

By 1949 the issues facing the nation were social and political. Cultural questions were either ignored in the face of the demands for revolutionary changes or answered in terms of a narrow Marxist-Leninist framework. Since the May Fourth Movement of 1919 traditional Chinese culture seemed to be on the way out and few bothered to take it seriously. Of course, in the villages popular culture remained, but at least with regard to this the Communist Party agreed with the missionaries that it was mere superstition. Nationalism, fueled by a desire to put an end to foreign domination, was a powerful force which in the circumstances of the time combined with hostility to 'feudal' thinking, and for most intellectuals this included religious ideas. Few Christians recognized the strength of the forces for change that brought about 'Liberation' and the triumph of the Communist Party. Inevitably, their response was uncertain and confused. Survival became the issue of the day, and Christians, understandably, differed as to the best way forward when faced by a government deeply hostile to all that Christians represented. It was in these circumstances that the Protestant Three Self Patriotic Movement (TSPM) was established. No wonder the

4. For further discussion see Whtye, op. cit., pp. 179-186. Also Ng Lee Ming, "The Promise and Limitations of Chinese Protestant Theologians, 1920-1950", *Ching Feng*, Vol 21 No 4, 1978. See also Dr. Winfried Gluer, *Christliche Theologie in China: T.C. Chao 1918-56*, Gutersloh: Gutersloher Verlagshaus Gerd Mohn, 1979.

problem of the relationship between culture and faith was entirely neglected at this period.

It is only since the Church emerged in 1979 from three decades of turmoil that Christians have begun to lead a relatively normal life. But the legacy of past years has meant that the 1980s were largely devoted to the task of rebuilding church life and this has absorbed much of their energy. In the meantime the official view of religion began to be modified. A debate started within academic circles on the question of whether religion should be described as an 'opiate', following the classical lines of Marxist Leninist interpretation, or whether religion should be seen, in certain circumstances, as a positive force within society. While there must still be many State officials who espouse the former interpretation, most Chinese social scientists would subscribe to the more liberal understanding, a view that came to have a certain degree of influence within the policy making organs of the Party and the State. This change in attitude towards religious questions reflected the break down of Marxist orthodoxy and a desire to search for new explanations.

The Contemporary Challenge

June 4th 1989 was a watershed. The doubts, the uncertainties of so many intellectuals in China concerning the Communist ideology were more than confirmed by the brutal suppression of all dissent. There can be no doubt that contemporary Chinese culture is in serious crisis, and the search for forms of cultural expression that are in some sense related to the best in Chinese tradition is now being pursued by many thoughtful Chinese.

At present, Christians are finding it hard to contribute to this debate in an explicit way. This is partly due to the continuing need to foster the internal life of the Church, but it is, in the main, the result of the nature of Chinese Christianity itself. While it appears probable that Christians are having some success in working out their relationship to the State there seems to be a serious question as to whether Christians can relate creatively to society and culture. The majority of Chinese believers are pietistic in outlook and are mainly concerned with the life and activity of the Church, rather than with the contribution Christians may be able to make to social development and political change. Such an attitude is not untypical of the life of the Church at certain phases in its history, but it tends to lead to accommodation with the State provided that the State is prepared to allow a certain degree of religious freedom, regardless of the political situation. For a variety of reasons Chinese Protestants who were influenced by the 'social gospel' in the 1920s and afterwards tended to align themselves with a leftist position that became more and more sympathetic to Marxism. The idealism and social concern of young Chinese intellectuals found its home in the Communist Party which by the late 1940s was regarded by people from all social classes as the best hope for a revived China. As events have unfolded in the past forty years Marxism has lost its appeal and those Christians who supported the New China of the 1950s must either cling to past assumptions or re-think their whole attitude.

Looked at in a simplistic, but not inaccurate way, one may distinguish three main groups within the Church: inward looking pietistic Christians represented both by people within the registered churches and meeting points and by unregistered meeting points; old-style 'Three Selfers' who continue to support the political status quo; and a group emerging from within the China Christian Council/Three Self Patriotic Movement who are increasingly aware of the need for significant political change in China. It was from this third group that support for the Democracy Movement of 1989 was forthcoming. Chinese Protestantism is therefore facing an urgent question concerning its attitude towards Chinese society. Many Christians see the question as one of good citizenship, but 'patriotism' in the light of the history of China since 1949 is a concept that demands more analysis than a mere accommodation to the powers that be. Confucian moral concern is apparent in the obvious fact that Christians are good workers, upright and honest citizens, but the fact has to be faced that by defining these activities and no others as 'patriotic' Christians are in danger of being subsumed under the banner of the CCP. Without doubt one reason for the policy of religious freedom is that Christians are seen as a force for stability in society. Insofar as the leaders of China are more concerned with stability than ideological orthodoxy, they will encourage the sort of Christianity that divides religious belief from politics.

The challenge is to discover the meaning of citizenship within the present totalitarian State that neither sells out to the State, nor leads to direct confrontation. Given the relative weakness of organized religion and the recent experiences of Christians in China, direct confrontation would not seem appropriate. Nevertheless a redefinition of 'patriotism' is necessary if Christians are to face the issue of the relationship of the Gospel to Chinese society. As they seek to assess the significance of the June '89 events only a very few are prepared to engage in what must ultimately be seen as an apologetic task. The apologia for Christianity in China in future years will need to be expressed in relationship to the political events of today. This is why the position taken by Bishop Ting (Ding Guangxun), President of the China Christian Council, is so important. He has been the most important Protestant leader in China for many years and it has been his careful and measured statesmanship that has given the Church room to breathe. He was in the 1950s one of those who supported the New China and until last June he continued to refrain from an open call for a reappraisal of the past. However, very quietly, he has been raising some critical questions with both the authorities and the Christian leadership itself. He has been the key figure in prompting a reassessment of priorities within the Church. It comes as no surprise, therefore, to discover that he has raised the question as to the meaning of 'patriotism' in contemporary China. In a recent comment he has referred to patriotism as 'affirming the best in the national tradition'. This is a significant shift away from the close linkage of 'patriotism' to support for the 'four basic principles' demanded by the CCP, which include supporting the leading role of the CCP itself[5].

5. Bishop Ting, verbal remarks to the British Council of Churches Delegation April/May 1990.

There are others who are taking a similar line, especially amongst younger Christian leaders. A young woman artist has commented that Christianity should be seen in relationship to culture and history rather than in relationship to political systems[6]. She sees herself exploring in her art the relations between faith and tradition, form and feeling. Whether consciously or not her ideas relate directly to the concerns raised by T.C. Chao. He was unable to resolve the contradiction between faith and political ideology, between political systems (form) and the freedom of the spirit (feeling), because in the context of revolution and national revival the past was experienced as a burden. Today, it is possible to put the events of 'Liberation' into a wider historical perspective in which it becomes clear that the communist political system is unable to maintain a creative tension between order and liberty and has succumbed to a sterile form clinging to a dead ideology. This is not to deny the importance of Marxism within the Chinese experience at a certain stage in its historical development, but it has become imperative to break the link between 'patriotism' and the Party. The past is once more open to be re-appropriated not by a mere restoration or revival but by a creative encounter. Here Christian faith can offer its prophetic critique of human systems and ideologies and by tackling the issue of the relationship of faith and tradition, form and feeling, make an important contribution in the search for new forms of cultural understanding in China.

The Integrity of the Church

An instructive parallel may be drawn from the history of the Church in South Korea. A very different political history has nevertheless produced some interesting similarities in the expression of Christian faith and in the cultural issues facing Christians[7].

There is first the close link between healing and conversion in both societies. This is not merely a rural phenomenon. Indeed one pastor in Shenyang, in the north-east of China, has indicated that up to 50% of conversions are the result of faith healing. We must take this very seriously if we are to understand the dynamics of popular Christianity in both China and Korea. Korean folk religion has roots in Siberian shamanism, a fact that differentiates it from Chinese folk religion, but both place considerable importance on faith healing and exorcism. The high value placed on miracle in traditional societies relates not only to the absence of modern medical facilities, but also to a view of the natural world and man's place within it which is radically different from the modern rationalistic understanding. Insofar as modern rationalism is itself a partial view of a complex universe, we cannot simply dismiss stories of healing, nor their importance within the religious growth of an individual or a community. At the same time, a mature faith is not dominated by wonder working, for Christian 'healing' has a

6. Verbal comments to BCC Delegation 1990.
7. The following remarks have been prompted by James Huntley Grayson's discussion of Korean Christianity in *Korea: A Religious History*, Oxford: Clarendon Press, 1989.

depth and a richness that reaches beyond the quest for mere physical healing towards that wholeness that can only be partially ours in this life. In both China and Korea there are many indications that a lack of a balanced view of healing is leading to serious distortions of the Gospel.
Secondly, the emphasis placed on material well being as one of the gifts of membership of the Christian Church is related in Korea to the traditional culture. The majority of Protestant Christians appear to believe that faith brings 'blessings' in the form of prosperity and the good life. In China too, such an emphasis fits neatly into traditional ideas, although it has not been elevated to the status of a doctrine. A recent visitor to Wenzhou City in Zhejiang was struck by the fact that in this stronghold of Protestantism in order to 'be anybody' it is necessary to be a Christian and that the largest and best buildings are churches. He found little evidence of a concern with social welfare or indeed with any social or political issues[8].
Thirdly, there are signs in China that the emphasis on 'growth' that has dominated Korean Christianity since the 1960s, is strong in some places. In South Korea growth is spectacular so that today it is reckoned that Christians form about one fifth of the population. In China Christians make up only around 1% of the population, but the phenomenon of rapid growth has appeared in certain areas (such as Wenzhou City). It is not impossible that this growth will extend to many parts of the country in the future. But in Korea there is much evidence to suggest that growth is leading to a loss of direction. According to James Grayson in his major study of Korean religion: "having achieved such outstanding numerical and physical success, the churches face the challenge of adapting themselves to this success without losing their commitment to the essence of Christianity[9]."

Towards a Critical Theology

Without a more critical element religion becomes subsumed in the values of traditional culture instead of engaging in a creative encounter with culture. On the surface this often leads to an overt denial of indigenous culture when in reality it is captive to the culture. James Grayson points to the links between 'Church Growth' and faith healing and the promise of 'blessings' in South Korea. He observes that "the direct Christian influence on Korean society and forms of cultural expression is disproportionately less than one would anticipate"[10].
Here we find both denial and accommodation resulting in a form and style of Christianity that is Western, but with a loss of authentic vision. It would be too much to say that this is what is happening in China, but the South Korean experience is a warning given the parallels we have discussed above. In fact, of

8. Unpublished report by Philip L. Wickeri, 1990.
9. Grayson, op. cit., p. 206.
10. Ibid., p. 207.

course, there is another side to Korean Christianity, expressed most forcefully in the movement to create an indigenous theology which began in the 1970s amongst overseas Korean Christians and imprisoned theologians in South Korea itself. The creation of the 'Minjung sinhak' or Theology of the People has been of enormous importance, not only for Korea[11]. It may well be of direct relevance to the Chinese situation, especially post June 4 when some Chinese are quietly speaking of the need for China's own version of Liberation Theology. Where then can we expect the impetus for such a development to emerge?

In the years before Liberation many intellectuals had shown interest in Christianity, but as we have suggested above, this tended to be replaced by Marxism. Over the past ten years a reverse phenomenon has been taking place. Commitment to Marxism is being replaced by interest in other value systems so that once more interest in Christianity in China is no longer confined to the Church. There is emerging amongst students and intellectuals the phenomenon of non-church Christians who come to faith through reading and personal reflection. On the whole they find life within the churches too constricting but they are in touch with some theologians within the Church. Most well known is Liu Xiaofeng who has been deeply influenced by Karl Barth. Liu is involved in the publication of a new journal, the Christian Cultural Review, the first issue of which appeared in early 1990[12]. Others include the artist Ding Fang, working in Beijing, and the writers An Shimeng and Liu Jing. There are many more intellectuals who are turning to Christianity as a source of inspiration, although not all would describe themselves as Christians. Bishop Ting is known to feel that such people may well be key figures in a new Chinese theology. Not limited by the traditional constraints of church life, they are working at that critical interface between theology and culture where creative thinking is most likely to emerge. The potential importance of this small group, linked to a few church based intellectuals, is far greater than their present influence might suggest.

It is, however, too early to bc sure of the significance of this development for the future of Christian apologetic in China. Such an apologia seems unlikely to arise from within the ranks of the Church itself without the stimulus provided by these outsiders. Yet if the Church is not to succumb to the dangers of cultural assimilation the growth of a critical theology is essential. There are certain interesting parallels with the 2nd century of the Christian era: a mass of Christians still essentially a Jewish sect, needed to justify their belief to the cultured pagan world of the Roman Empire. It was the role of the 'Apologists' such as Justin Martyr and Tertullian to develop an adequate Christian theological response to pagan philosophy. In China Marxism does not provide a serious intellectual challenge, but the diffuse and largely unacknowledged matrix of thought that somehow still constitutes a peculiarly 'Chinese' response to the world does present such a challenge to faith. At no time in the past has the possibility of a crea-

11. For discussion of Minjung Theology see Christian Conference of Asia *Minjung Theology: People as Subjects of History*, Maryknoll: Orbis, 1983; also Jung Young Lee, (ed.) *An Emerging Theology in World Perspective*, Mystic, Conneticut: Twenty Third Publications, 1988.
12. *Christian Cultural Review*, Guiyang, 1990.

tive encounter confronted Christians so clearly. How they respond may well determine the whole future of Christianity in China.

Church Unity

We move now to deal with the complex problem of the understanding of the Church within Chinese Protestantism. The legacy of the missionary movement was one of a Church divided into many denominations. There were, of course, significant attempts at unification, the most important being the formation of the Church of Christ in China in 1927. There were also the creation of indigenous sects such as the Little Flock and the True Jesus Church, modelled on similar Western sectarian movements but rejecting direct missionary involvement. Missionaries from mainline Protestant churches frequently found that their converts were uninterested in matters of ecclesiology with the result that a kind of 'congregational' understanding of the Church tended to predominate even amongst those related to Methodist or Reformed traditions. The Little Flock, with its doctrine of one local church in each place, merely took this tendency to its extreme. Despite this legacy, it may also be said that 'unity' appeals to many Chinese Christians who fail to understand the subtle distinctions between the denominations within the Western Church and the accompanying theological and ecclesiological differences. But in another way there has been a failure to set 'unity' within a catholic understanding of the Church with the result that unity has been seen largely as a matter relating to the local church.

A further complication has been provided by the isolation of local churches and of individual Christians due to political upheavals over the past forty years. This has made it even harder for a catholic understanding to develop and has resulted in considerable fragmentation which has fostered disunity even between local congregations. It must also be remembered that over this whole period the authorities have sought to control religious life at all levels, and that the slogan of 'unity' has been used as one of the most potent means of control, most notably in the late 1950s when many local churches merged. While this was in part the result of declining membership it was mainly due to the leftist political climate during the disastrous 'Great Leap Forward' of 1958/59. This was itself a precursor of the Cultural Revolution when the only Church was, in the words of one Chinese Christian, the "church in our hearts".

After the initial fervour of the Cultural Revolution died down it was possible for limited Christian activities to re-emerge in 1971/2 and from 1976 the Church began to grow rapidly. It was a creative and exciting period, but the isolation and the lack of formal structures led in many places to an over reliance on the memories of older believers and to a dependence on charismatic local leaders. Other objective factors such as city/rural divisions, poor communications, semi-literacy, and lack of resources have all helped to keep Christians apart. Rapid growth in numbers in such a situation can bring all the problems discussed in the previous section of this paper. It is not without reason that Bishop

"Episcopacy w/out diocesan organization?"

Ting speaks of the present time as a critical moment in the history of Chinese Christianity.

Unity versus diversity is therefore an urgent issue that faces the Church. Unfortunately, there is a tendency within the leadership to see unity in terms of centralization and control rather than as a theological concept concerning the nature of the Church. Tradition in both its Confucian and Communist manifestations reinforces these authoritarian attitudes. Fear of stepping out of line, inertia, organizational experience, all make it difficult for church officials to adjust to a more relaxed pluralistic outlook. On the other hand the existence of large numbers of Christians who have no developed theology of the Church represents a serious problem for church leaders aware of the need for a national united church structure. This need relates to the avoidance of heresy and the fostering of congregations with few financial and human resources, but above all to the recognition of an essential oneness in Christ that demands the development of a catholic ecclesiology in some form. The actual form of this unity is open – Bishop Ting hopes for a 'congregational/presbyterian' structure but with bishops seen as related to the historic episcopate of the Church.

The problem was raised at the Fourth National Christian Conference in 1986 but no agreement was reached. In June 1988 two bishops were consecrated in Shanghai by the Municipal Christian Council, but so far this has not been imitated elsewhere. In the second century it was the bishop who provided the focus for unity. China would seem to be in need of such a focus, vested in representative persons respected for their experience and insight. This might suggest a form of episcopacy but one which avoids a diocesan organization. This is the pattern that has been adopted in Shanghai.

Church Organization

We turn at this point to a consideration of the present organization of Protestantism in China. Obviously it is not strictly possible to speak of a Protestant Church, rather of a federation of local churches operating through the two national Christian organizations and their provincial equivalents. The development of public structures in 1979/80 after a gap of thirteen years or more enabled Christians to start to organize themselves once again. However, the TSPM, while acting as a useful bridge between government and Church showed as time went on that it was unable to adapt sufficiently to changing circumstances. The newly created China Christian Council was not given sufficient independence and many Christians resent the political control exercised by the Religious Affairs Bureau of the State Council and the United Front Work Department of the CCP. Nevertheless, the 1980s saw a gradual relaxation of the pressure with the consequent emergence of a less controlled and more authentic search for Christian unity. This was accompanied by continued church growth in an atmosphere of economic reform, especially evident in the countryside where the abolition of the commune and the reversion to farming by households has encouraged greater freedom and has enabled many church workers to devote considerable time to church related activities. One inevitable result of the limited liberalization of political life in both rural and urban areas has been an increase in the pressures for greater diversity of expression.

The powerful Little Flock tradition most clearly represents the trend towards such diversity. It is creating strains within the present monolithic structures that are bound either to lead to the re-emergence of denominations or to a new understanding of diversity within a unified organization. The strain is reinforced by bad political experiences in the past and the ambiguities of TSPM practice which continue in some areas today. Already, the Seventh Day Adventists are well on the way to creating their own distinct denominational structure, in this case encouraged from outside. If the Little Flock and True Jesus Church are to be encouraged to cooperate more enthusiastically with the China Christian Council, then it will be necessary for the TSPM to give up its control over church affairs. Unity can no longer be seen as monolithic and the old slogan "seeking the common ground while reserving differences" will have to be properly implemented[13].

Since the Third National Christian Conference in 1980 and the creation of the China Christian Council, the TSPM has had no legitimate reason for continuing to exercise ecclesiastical jurisdiction. However, the legacy of past years has meant that the TSPM has been reluctant to give up its power. Its organization and work style are rooted in the 1950s and the political context in which one Party claims a monopoly of power. What may have been appropriate in one period ceases to be so in another and the TSPM is, in the opinion of most Christians an increasing barrier to the normalization of church life. What, we may then ask, is the future of the Three Self Patriotic Movement and how will it relate to the China Christian Council? Following on from this is the further question of the nature and role of the CCC itself.

The leadership is itself deeply divided on this question. On the one hand there are hard line 'leftists' some of whom, at least, genuinely believe that without socialist education, the church is lost. On the other hand there are leaders like Bishop Ting who recognize that times have changed and who wish to separate the CCC from TSPM control. As he has stated recently, "If Christ is the Head of the Church, there should not be another head over the Church"[14]. It is certain that here he is in tune with the thoughts of ordinary Christians, even if in the present political climate he faces an uphill struggle within the TSPM/CCC leadership. The 'leftist' view was able to regain the initiative in the autumn of 1989 as a result of the June events, but there are already indications that the forthcoming Joint National Committee of the CCC/TSPM will insist that the TSPM be restricted to fulfilling the role of political liaison laid down in its constitution[15].

13. For a detailed treatment of this theme see Philip L. Wickeri, *Seeking the Common Ground, Protestant Christianity, the Three Self Movement and China's United Front*, Maryknoll: Orbis, 1988.
14. Bishop K.H. Ting in conversation with the BCC Delegation April/May 1990.
15. The Joint Committee in fact met in August 1990 and reversed the liberal trend, reasserting the supervisory role of the TSPM. Rumours of a more rigid religious policy being promulgated from the government surfaced during the summer and were confirmed in the autumn.

Pressures on the Church have increased since June 1989 but in the main these have followed the classical path of restricting unrecognized activities. Such public but unofficial activities always exist in a grey hinterland in which nothing is clearly defined and therefore the limits to 'religious freedom' shift with the overall political climate. Other factors are present within a given situation: regional and provincial loyalties and rivalries; 'connections' between alumni or blood relatives to name just two important ones. Prior to June 1989 a Religious Law was under preparation and a delegation of government officials visited Western Europe in April/May of that year to look at Church/State relations. Zhang Shenzuo, deputy Director of the United Front Work Department of the CCP, and deputy leader of the delegation, when asked to comment on progress in drafting the law, was noticeably vague in his response[16]. Yet, without such a law believers will never quite know where they stand.

There are still many State officials who wish to curb all activities not directly run under the auspices of the CCC/TSPM and too many TSPM personnel are prepared to cooperate with them. At the same time, certain leaders are showing an increasing tendency to support the right of independent meeting points to exist. The recent closure of Pastor Lin Xian'gao's meeting point in Guangzhou suggests that control over unofficial Christian groups is tightening, especially in areas that showed a leftist tendency before the events of June 1989[17]. While the present political climate continues the situation is likely to grow worse.

There are a number of huge issues here. It must be doubted if the more sectarian parts of the Church can be brought into a meaningful united Church. The innate congregationalism of many local churches is unlikely to disappear. There is then the problem of developing a genuinely pluralistic form of church life in an authoritarian society. What is 'religious freedom' in a context in which the Religious Affairs Bureau defines the meaning of 'normal' religious activities? Until these political questions can be tackled in an open way it is doubtful if any really fundamental change can be made in the way that public Christian life functions. The pressures for change will continue to grow, especially as younger leaders begin to assume responsibility. As the 1990s progress so a leadership crisis will develop. Let us turn to look briefly at this problem.

Leadership Transition

The problem of making a change to a new and younger leadership is focused at the present time in the question of the role of young Christians trained in the new colleges and Bible schools and now graduating. There is a reluctance to ac-

16. Meeting at the United Front Work Department, Beijing, with members of the BCC Delegation, April/May 1990.
17. Suppression of home meetings and tighter controls on religious bodies spread in late 1990. Bishop Ting spoke against this at the September meeting of the National Peoples Congress Standing Committee and at the TSPM/CCC Joint Committee in August. Bishop Shen Yifan's speech at the Joint Committee revealed a hardening of attitude, despite Bishop Ting's outspoken criticisms. *Tianfeng*, November 1990.

cept young people as leaders at the local level, partly from tradition, partly from a refusal by the old guard to let go. Nationally, there are a few outstanding graduates of the Jinling Seminary, some of whom have trained initially in regional colleges, who are taking on a leadership role, but it remains to be seen how widely they will be accepted. Local churches are often suspicious of what they see as 'liberal' theology and there is also suspicion of the political purity of students post June 1989 by the State authorities.

Many of the thousands of voluntary church workers are from the middle generation which is so missing in the ranks of the pastorate. More acceptable than young graduates, these workers represent the key to a successful leadership transition. The recent setting up of a correspondence course by the Jinling Seminary with about 1000 members is an important step towards providing adequate training. The year long courses offered at Jinling and in other seminaries are also ways of training these leaders, many of whom have emerged as the natural leaders of their congregations.

The transition to a younger national leadership will be difficult. As Bishop Ting reaches his mid-seventies, so the question of a successor becomes more acute. There are few obvious choices. Most provincial leaders are also over 70. Zhao Fusan, once mentioned as a possible successor, is in exile. Bishop Shen Yifan of Shanghai is perhaps the only candidate who might be acceptable to both sides in the debate over the organization of the Church, but this is by no means certain. It is possible that a collective form of leadership will be necessary, but its effectiveness must be in doubt. There are certainly some excellent younger leaders in certain provinces but they are not well known outside of their province and do not have the breadth of experience of a man like Bishop Ting. It will be interesting to see how this matter is resolved.

Economic Problems

Financial problems stemming from inflation, the need to pay new pastors (many elderly pastors received pensions from the State), the end of income from reparations after the Cultural Revolution are causing a serious problem for the CCC. Churches in poorer areas are unable to sustain full time pastors. In places with few Christians it is difficult to provide church buildings and there are insufficient resources for training, materials etc. These economic constraints have prompted a re-thinking of the three self principles. The recent opening of a Theological Education Fund and the request to overseas donors represents a new evaluation of the meaning of 'self support'. Pressures on local churches to seek support from overseas are considerable (and understandable). Yet, there are serious questions to be asked about the wisdom of going too far down this road.

Relationships With Catholics

Before drawing our conclusions, it is important to remind ourselves that the discussion has been solely concerned with non-Roman Catholic Christians. The relationship between Protestants and Catholics in China is insignificant at present, but in the long term each has a lot to offer the other. As we have seen, Chinese Protestantism lacks the effective ecclesiology it needs to come to terms with the 'catholic' nature of the Church as this has been understood within the Christian mainstream since the early centuries of the Church. Chinese Catholics are entrenched in pre-Vatican II attitudes and need to breathe the spirit of reform. The failure to relate in a significant way is harming both churches. The 'Inculturation' of theology may in the end be the means of bringing the two into meaningful dialogue. For the present the whole issue is too remote from the immediate concerns of either group to have a priority status. It is important, however, not to lose sight of it.

Conclusion

These are just some of the most critical questions facing Chinese Protestants today. The Tiananmen massacre and its aftermath have exacerbated many of the outstanding problems but they were all there before that event. Lest this picture should appear to suggest that the situation of the Protestant Church in China is a gloomy one, let me finish with a positive evaluation of the long term future for Christianity in China.

First of all on the organizational level: just as the question of democratization will not go away in Chinese society as a whole so the Church cannot avoid it in its own life. The old style of organization cannot last. Behind the scenes the opposition is building and has the support of key leaders both locally and nationally.

Second on the question of unity: pluralism may lead to increased fragmentation but it will also bring a more genuine unity to many Christians and it will encourage freedom of discussion which can only result in a healthy theological debate in which outstanding issues can at last be addressed. So, turning from preoccupations with survival Christians will look at Chinese culture in a new light. All Chinese will face the task of cultural renewal and reconstruction 'after Marxism' and Christianity is already showing that it has a major contribution to make, even if this may come in part at least from non-Church Christians.

Third, whatever problems may afflict local churches, they are in the overwhelming majority of places subsidiary to the vitality of spiritual life, representing a positive force within an increasingly difficult economic and political environment. It is this rich and profound experience that any perceptive visitor to the Chinese Church soon becomes aware of. It is this that represents the true potential of Chinese Christianity in the next century.

5. A YEAR OF CONFRONTATION: THE CATHOLIC CHURCH IN CHINA IN 1989

Edmond Tang

When I was asked in early 1989 to draft a report on the situation of the Catholic Church in China I gave it the following title: "The Catholic Church in China – seen through a kaleidoscope". The players in the field were clearly distinguishable but their positions were constantly changing and none of them had yet to dominate the field of action. The picture of the Catholic Church was very different depending on the angle from which the viewer looked at the situation. There were, first of all, the 'patriots' and the 'faithful'. However, more and more of the 'patriots' were openly declaring their allegiance to the Pope, and among the 'faithful' many found working with the government-sponsored Patriotic Association an acceptable modus vivendi. On the other hand a new group, calling itself the 'underground Church', was emerging with a clear confrontational posture. The Vatican, worried about the unbridled growth of the underground hierarchy, tried to moderate their posture and sought with a new urgency to normalize the situation. Also for the first time a group of bishops, acceptable to both the Chinese government and the Vatican, was increasing in number and becoming an important factor in solving the long-standing Sino-Vatican conflict. Even well-placed observers admitted there was confusion:

> "Even the closest observers of the Church in China are bewildered by the strange and contradictory stories which they are hearing. In one place a church which had been destroyed is being rebuilt thanks to government money; elsewhere Christians are building a church and reject government assistance; in still another place Catholics refuse to accept a bishop without papal approval. In some churches believers will make their confession to one priest but refuse to accept another. Some bishops of the independent Church, which refuses to accept the authority of Rome, openly attack the authority of the successor of Peter; other bishops of the same independent organization send secret messages of loyalty to the Pope. Certain elderly priests work together with official bodies; others chose to return to prison rather than join a Church which they consider apostate. A married 'patriotic' bishop dies and his priests refuse to give him a religious burial. In a provincial city one priest preaches loyalty to Rome; in another city a priest is frightened to receive foreign visitors. In some areas only the priests know who the bishop is: the believers are not told for fear that someone will betray him[1]."

1. Laszlo Ladany, "Reflexion sur l'Eglise en Chine", *Commentaire* 1988, p. 640.

Another commentator notes that "three bishops visited on the same day may represent three realities of the Church: the underground, those approved by both the Holy See and the Government, and the open, official one, realities that are part of the complex spectrum of the Church in China[2]."

Amidst this confusion there were certain patterns emerging but the whole situation was also fluid and changing with its hopes and inherent dangers. On the one hand the establishment of relations between the Vatican and China was said to be imminent. The visit of Cardinal Jaime Sin of Manila to China in November 1987 and his high level discussions with Zhao Ziyang, the Premier and Secretary-general of the Party at the time, led many to ask the question: how much longer will it be before China establishes normal diplomatic relations with the Vatican, the only state in Europe which still does not recognize the People's Republic? In fact low key official conversations had been going on for some time. This speculation was reinforced by the changes in China itself. A new religious law was drafted and circulated which would eventually normalize the rights of religions in Chinese society. The hierarchy of leadership in the Catholic Church was redefined in a series of declarations which put the authority of the Bishops' Conference and the Church Affairs Commission above that of the Chinese Catholic Patriotic Association (CCPA). The latter had always dominated the internal as well as the external affairs of the Church since its creation in 1957. These changes seem to meet one of the Vatican's conditions that for the establishment of normal relations the Catholic Church in China must be directed by a proper religious authority. Although it may be questioned whether this transfer of authority was as effective as it sounded it cannot be denied that many bishops had openly asserted their authority in the previous couple of years. Institutionally the pastoral and theological concerns had also been taken up by the Bishops' Conference and commissions were established to study the reform of the liturgy, theological concerns such as 'inculturation' of the faith, theological training of future priests, etc.

It is important to mention that in the same declarations, both by the government and by the Church, it was recognized for the first time that spiritual affiliation with the Holy See did not necessarily contradict loyalty to the country. In fact some bishops, illicitly consecrated in the past, had been privately reconciled with the Vatican.

Despite this rosy picture we have just painted, the dark clouds were never completely absent from the horizon. The growth of the underground Church was worrying. After years of silence it had surfaced with an organized strength which could not be underestimated. Its style was becoming openly hostile and its influence was spreading, creating confusion among Catholic communities. To counter this 'disruptive' development the CCPA was returning to repressive measures.

Many still believed in 1989 that there was some hope of changing the situation through dialogue and bridge-building by moderate groups both inside and

2. Ismael Zuloaga, "The actual situation of the Catholic Church in China", paper presented to the European China Meeting, Rhondorf, Germany 16-18 November, 1988.

below – explicit challenge / confrontation by U.C.

outside China. The Vatican too, after years of encouraging the development of the underground Church became concerned about the negative developments and sent in a series of directives with the hope of clarifying the situation.

1989 – a year of confrontation

By spring 1989, events in China had taken a dramatic turn and the pattern that emerged was more and more one of open confrontation. At a time when a solution seemed to be at hand, schism became also a real possible outcome. The determining factor seemed to be the growth of an underground Catholic Church whose strength and tenacity had up to this point been underestimated.
Throughout 1989 there were a number of large and small confrontations and the underground Church was involved in almost all the cases. For the purpose of illustration it suffices to mention two here:
1) In April 1989 in a place called Youtong, about 30 kilometres south of Shijiazhuang in Hebei province, a group of underground Catholics had taken over a local school campus and erected a tent as a church. The school was built on grounds where a church had once stood before it was destroyed.
After a series of fruitless exchanges the government raided the place on 18 April. It was reported that two persons were killed in the melée and 350 were wounded with 30 arrests. The Youtong Catholics then disseminated pamphlets, with the help of University students from Shandong province, in Tiananmen Square accusing the government of violating their religious freedom and using force against them. On 23 June, 300 armed police came again to the campus and demolished the tent.
2) Since November 1989 there had been several waves of arrests. The immediate cause was a secret meeting in Zhangyi, Shaanxi province on 21 November which brought together a number of underground Bishops. The purpose of the meeting was to set up an alternative Bishops' Conference. This was a direct challenge to the legitimacy of the existing official Bishops' Conference created in 1981. From December 1989 to February 1990 there was a sequence of arrests. Among the 30 or so clergy detained were 6 Bishops from Gansu, Hebei, Shaanxi and Inner Mongolia.
These arrests signify a different level of confrontation between the government, the Patriotic Association and the so-called underground Church. The arrests could no longer be considered as individual cases of conscience or individuals having trespassed the official line. What was involved was a growing campaign by a group of Catholics in a series of co-ordinated actions against the open Churches under the administration of the Patriotic Association.
These incidents, given their scale and significance, should have attracted greater attention from the international press which reported them only in passing. This is not surprising since these incidents took place either during the turbulent pro-democracy movement in China or in its aftermath. They were also overshadowed by the dramatic turn of events in Eastern Europe.
Several questions come to our minds when we try to analyse the growing conflict:

How far are the confrontations involving the Catholic Church, especially the arrests since November 1989, related to the crushing of the pro-democracy movement of June 1989?
Does this concern only the Catholic Church or are the Protestant Churches equally affected?
To what extent does this represent a shift of the government's religious policy, not so much in theoretical terms, but in its practical application?
Why were those confrontations coming to a head in 1989? What are the likely scenarios for the Catholic Church if the conflicts continue to increase?

Repercussions of the June 4 incident

The events of June 4 did not leave the Churches untouched. First of all, with the growing identification of the Churches with the social problems of the country, some Christians and theological students took an active part in the pro-democracy movement both in Beijing and Nanjing. Some Christian leaders were involved too, with some of them giving support to the cause of the students and joining with other members of the People's Congress to oppose the declaration of martial law.
After 4 June all organizations in China were under pressure to support the government. Understandably both Catholic and Protestant institutions issued public statements supporting the government's actions, if not denouncing the pro-democracy movement directly. Some Church leaders had to re-interpret their earlier statements. All over the country, churches felt obliged to hold prayer services for the victims of the June events, victims here meaning the soldiers who died on duty. Donations were also collected for the soldiers' families. Seminarians were asked to sign statements concerning their whereabouts and attitude vis-a-vis the pro-democracy movement; some refused to sign and were denied ordination.
The June events were not taken lightly by the Chinese authorities in spite of reassuring statements to the contrary. Throughout the latter half of 1989 Party/security officials were sent down from Beijing to all provinces to settle accounts with cadres and work units which were suspected for their sympathy with the students. Important cadres, including those in the Churches, were said to be under internal criticism for their stance during the June events. Although the policy of religious freedom was maintained officially it is questionable whether the leaders of the Church who were sympathetic to the pro-democracy movement could still exercise an effective leadership. It is also clear that there were divisions within the Churches regarding the proper attitude they should assume. In short, if the official policy had not changed, and in fact the government had allowed more overseas visits of Chinese Church leaders to restore their international relations, nevertheless it is certain that the reins are getting tighter for the religions in China. Unofficial activities, such as those of some house gatherings as well as those of the underground Catholic Church, will no longer be tolerated. The official tone has become harsher as well.

The Underground Catholic Church

On the other hand it is not possible to make a direct link between the June events and the growing conflicts involving the Catholic Church. In fact these conflicts have a history dating back to before the rise of the pro-democracy movement. The harsh response of the Chinese authorities was also expressed in an earlier policy document as we shall discuss later. The single important factor which brought the confrontations to a head was the emergence of a militant underground Catholic Church.

Before we attempt to discuss the situation any further, it may be useful to provide a few details about the so-called Underground Church and its evolution in the past few years. What, or more exactly, who is the underground Church? When speaking of the underground Church it is perhaps useful to distinguish between two moments of its history.

There are first of all the Catholics who in the 1950s, following the instruction of the Holy See, refused to join or recognize the leadership for the Chinese Patriotic Association. They refused to go to the open churches or to accept the sacraments administered by pastors who had joined the Association. These Catholics therefore practised their faith privately in homes and were served by itinerant priests. Although hostile to the open churches, their attitude was more defensive in character.

Many came out of the Cultural Revolution accepting the more open government policy and recognized the changes within the Patriotic Association itself. Some changed their attitude and agreed to work within the framework of the Patriotic Association although they did not share its extreme position towards the Vatican.

The underground Church that is often talked about in the 1980s is of a different character; being more organized and more aggressive, the concern of the leaders is not only a pastoral one, seeking for alternative ways of serving Catholics who do not want to worship in open Churches. Their activities become more and more daring and seem to suggest that they are seeking a confrontation with the existing authorities. Secretly ordained priests have been sent all over the country denouncing others who had joined the Patriotic Association and instructing Catholics not to receive sacraments from the latter since they are considered to be invalid. Many communities have become confused and divided by actions of these priests and their denunciations.

It is undeniable that the present underground Church took shape in late 1979 when the Vatican gave a series of exemptions to the underground pastors so that religious life could be practised without following the canonical laws of the Church. Most of the exemptions concerned the canonical regulations for the effective celebration of the sacraments. However, following repeated requests from the ageing bishops and priests who were worried about their succession, the Vatican also granted permission to ordain priests without the required seminary training. Permission was also given to the ageing bishops to nominate and consecrate their successors, and this power was even extended to the choosing of bishops for neighbouring dioceses without bishops.

This extra-canonical permission was seen by some as the green light to build a Church in opposition. The first secret bishops were consecrated in 1981. According to a confidential document there were at least fifty such consecrations by the end of 1989: eight in 1981, thirteen in 1982, four in 1983, five in 1984, three in 1985, one in 1986, five in 1987, one in 1988 and ten in 1989.

In fact the real figure might be much higher because there were consecrations which only came to the notice of the Vatican much later on. Numerous priests were ordained secretly. It seems that the consecrations and ordinations were already far beyond the original pastoral intentions of the Vatican permissions.

Even persons close to the position of the Vatican have expressed their disquiet regarding recent developments. They admit that some of the newly consecrated bishops did not have sufficient pastoral experience, and in some cases they did not have a good working relationship with other priests. As for the privately-ordained priests, many were very young and had received minimal doctrinal instruction. Some were known more for their zeal for denouncing others than for their pastoral skills. The result was the birth of a militant opposition which put the new atmosphere of dialogue in jeopardy.

Divisions in the Church

What characterizes this new underground Church? Not only is it antagonistic to the open Churches, but it is more and more open and aggressive in its tactics. The little black priests as they were often called because of their operation in secret, were sent to different provinces from Hebei up to the remotest parishes to mobilize the faithful against the open churches. They say that the Patriotic Association is the work of the devil ("love your enemies but not the devil" they would say), and that the sacraments administered by priests belonging to it are invalid and ineffective. In fact it would be better to abstain from the sacraments than commit another mortal sin. . . . .

The source of this information of the underground Church is contained in a document called "The Thirteen Points" attributed to Bishop Fan Xueyan of Baoding[3]. Bishop Fan had always been a staunch opponent of the Patriotic Association and had endured long imprisonment and police surveillance for his beliefs. His closeness to the Vatican also lends authority to his views. Since its circulation in September 1988, the effect of the "Thirteen Points" was devastating. Churches once full are now emptied. And the faithful have been thrown into confusion.

An example is the diocese of Xianxian in Hebei province. Xianxian is a traditional Catholic stronghold, as are many dioceses of Hebei. Christians there suffered much during the Boxer Uprising of 1900 and the Sino-Japanese War. The conflicts of the 1950s have also left their mark.

After the Cultural Revolution many of the priests who had formerly been im-

3. Different versions of this document circulate in China. An English translation can be found in the transcript of Radio Veritas Broadcasts (undated).

prisoned for their opposition to the Patriotic Association welcomed the new religious freedom. They recognized the positive developments in the Association, especially those which did not follow the position of the National Association in Beijing. In some places, such as Xianxian a modus vivendi was found which allowed pastors faithful to the Vatican to operate within the framework of the Association. This, however, was not acceptable to the underground group of Christians.

Recently Xianxian diocese was visited by a Catholic Bishop from Taiwan, himself a native of Hebei. It was his first visit since the change of regime on the mainland. In a report written after the visit he expressed his painful observation of the division in the diocese: the major problem of the area, according to this Taiwan bishop, was the dissension sown by the underground priests:

> "In the Diocese of Xianxian, the Church is very much alive. In the diocese there are 26 priests and 100 sisters. There is also a seminary with 60 seminarians from 18 to 20 years of age. Between 1985 and 1989 70 churches had been built... His Excellency, Joannes Liu Dinghan and all the priests (11 Jesuits and 15 diocesan priests) work very hard even if they have been constantly misunderstood by the neighbouring diocese of Baoding[4]. The latter says that Bishop Liu Dinghan belongs to the Patriotic Church. Bishop Joannes Liu and his priests have, nevertheless, publicly declared their obedience to the Holy Father. Moreover, in every church of Xianxian Diocese, the faithful pray for the Holy Father, for all bishops, priests and the universal Church[5]."

In the same diocese there was also an underground bishop, a Rev. X, who refused to cooperate with Bishop Liu and accused Liu of having been excommunicated by the Pope, without knowing that Liu had been legitimized by the Vatican. This bishop, isolated from other priests and Christians, ordained on his own some ten young priests after only a few months of study. These young priests were more specialized in acts of denunciations and 'knowledge' about excommunications than in the doctrines of the Church or pastoral work among the faithful. They publicly denounced other pastors and preached that sacraments administered by the 'patriots' were invalid. As for those who had been baptized or married by 'patriotic priests' they must be re-baptized and re-married. This state of affairs is not limited to Xianxian or Hebei alone. In fact the influence of the underground Church is widespread, from Gansu and Inner Mongolia to Shaanxi, Shanxi, and Hebei to Liaoning in the northeast and Fujian in the southeast. The Taiwan bishop's report concluded that:

> "The Holy See must come out with sanctions and regulations to ensure that underground bishops do not unnecessarily ordain new bishops and priests who do not meet the requirements for the priesthood. These 'little black

4. The diocese of Bishop Fan, who was supposed to have issued the "Thirteen Points".
5. An unpublished report widely circulated in English.

priests', so-called by the Christians, do not spread the Gospel; instead, they foster hate among the faithful. They do not preach God's word; instead, they engage in name-calling and labeling other people. Obviously, the Church is divided; hence, the Christians are scandalized and have no wish to go to the church. This sad situation exists in several places[6]."

The situation, indeed, is not limited to Hebei province. For example in a certain diocese of Inner Mongolia there are three bishops in one place each claiming legitimate authority over the same territory. One is a secret bishop only recently known to the Vatican. Another is a bishop who had reconciled with Rome without the underground bishop knowing it. The antagonism that exists between the protagonists has practically paralysed the whole diocese and divided the Catholic community.

Government responses

Officially the Catholic Church in China is an independent Church, and the Chinese constitution stipulates that no religious body can be dominated by a foreign power. Yet it is commonly acknowledged that over the last couple of years in many Churches, including those in Shanghai and other prominent cities, Christians pray openly for the Pope. More and more Church leaders have declared themselves united with the Holy See without necessarily attracting the ire of the authorities. In the case of Xianxian mentioned above it is common practice. The residing bishop has been reconciled with the Vatican. In the churches of the diocese the pictures of John Paul II are exhibited and prayers are said for him. Does this development represent a change of position in the government's policy in dealing with the Catholic Church?

A recent document seems to suggest this possibility. Document no. 3, entitled "Directives of the Party on how to deal with the Catholic Church in the new situation", issued by the Party Central Committee and the State Council in April 1989, recommends to the cadres a policy of differentiation in dealing with Catholics. Article 4 of the document says: "Pay attention to differentiate the underground forces from those clergy who are separated from us because of their faith in the Pope[7]."

The 'new situation' that the document refers to could be the promising negotiations leading up to the eventual establishment of diplomatic relations with the Vatican. For some time a moderate or intermediate group between the staunch 'patriots' and the 'underground Catholics' has been accepted and even promoted in view of this new situation. In the same document the authority of the Bishops' Conference over that of the Patriotic Association is recognized. The rights of the Churches to their former property have also been extended from the actual church buildings to the land and associated buildings they owned.

6. Ibid.
7. *China Catholic Communication*, January 1990, pp. 3-5.

On the other hand the 'new situation' may also be referring to the growing strength of the underground Church. The document recommends the cadres to deal with all underground activities sternly. This is in line with the regulations issued by provincial authorities in e.g. Guangdong and Hebei. These regulations gave exclusive rights to groups recognized by the government while calling for "the elimination of Catholic underground religious activities". According to the Hebei regulations it is stipulated that only the clergy and their activities recognized by the national Bishops' Conference and the provincial Catholic Church Affairs Commission will be protected by law; those without recognition will not be allowed to conduct religious activities. In the same vein, only the training centres officially run by the dioceses are protected; those without such permission should be dissolved.

Many analysts interpret this document as having two objectives: 1) to eradicate the influence of the underground Church, and 2) to give exclusive legal rights and financial support to an autonomous Catholic Church and to make this a fait accompli before the establishment of relations with Rome. Whatever the major objective of the directives of Document 3, it is certain that the underground Church will become the target of mounting pressures from the government. The use of force in the Youtong incident in April 1989 and the arrests of dissident clergy from December 1989 to February 1990 seem to bear this out.

New Attitudes of the Official Church

On the other hand the official Church is also positioning itself for the 'new situation'. A meeting of the National Bishops' Conference was held in March 1989 in which certain new positions were adopted, namely:

1) The Pope must be recognized as the Head of the Church and Catholics must be allowed to pray for him.

2) The Bishops' Conference should assume the leadership of the Church and not the Patriotic Association which should function only under the Conference.

3) Bishops who are known to be married should no longer be members of the Bishops' Conference or the Church Affairs Commission.

Similar questions were raised at a meeting of the Church Affairs Commission which was held at the end of April. In that meeting the Bishops reaffirmed their position that it was the Bishops' Conference that was the primary holder of responsibility for the administration of the dioceses.

As for relations with the Holy See, the Bishops had this to say: "Our faith-relationship with the Holy See has never been cut off. What has been cut off is the political relationship which prevents us from having the external contacts with the Holy See. Our faith remains the same as before."

This affirmation of the spiritual leadership of the Pope is in line with some of the statements made by individual bishops in the past few years. Instead of looking for alternative theological arguments, which was the case in the early 1980s, the same bishop-theologians are returning to the traditional ecclesiological position of the Catholic Church.

Some China analysts are sceptical about the ecclesiological assertion of the Bishops' authority, knowing the domination of the Patriotic Association in the past in the affairs of the Church. However, it should not be forgotten that a similar trend is taking place in the Protestant Churches as well. The China Christian Council is also asserting its authority over the Three Self Movement and this seems to have received the support of the United Front Department itself.

It is of course questionable whether the Patriotic Association has changed its fundamental attitude. On the other hand it cannot be denied that some internal changes have taken place in these last years. Firstly there is a growing difference between the national association in Beijing and the provincial ones. Some of the latter have gradually moved to more open positions and under their umbrella religious activities have returned to normal. In some places they have been openly criticized and discarded by the local Bishop. In other instances they were challenged by the local Bishop to revise their views and strategies in order to catch up with the changing moods of the majority of Christians. Despite certain attitudes emanating from Beijing, it is no longer feasible to treat the Patriotic Associations as a monolithic bloc which does not respond to the changing tide.

Concluding Observations

It should become clear from the above account of the recent developments of the Catholic Church in China, that the emergence of the underground Church has tilted the traditional balance and holds the key to any solution in the future. It must be remembered here that the emergence of the underground Catholic Church finds a certain parallel in the Protestant house gatherings. Although not as militant and organized as the Catholic underground, there are groups in the Protestant Churches which escape the jurisdiction of the China Christian Council and would prefer to remain so. This suggests an important consideration: that the division in the Catholic Church cannot be reduced simply to a dispute over loyalty to the Holy See. There must be sociological factors which are common to both these Catholic and Protestant dissenting groups.

There are a number of questions which are of particular interest:

To what extent has the Cultural Revolution changed the organizational patterns or power relations within the Church and made the growth of dissenting or parallel groups possible?

How far is the emergence of these groups related to the revival of popular religions now documented by social scientists? In fact popular Christianity is characterized by practices of healing, miracles, etc. which echo some of the practices of the folk religions. Are there common aspects in their rural background, figuration of deities and emphasis on magical rituals?

What are the patterns of conversion and what are the determining factors for the growth of underground or parallel groups? Why are they more effective, in some cases, than the official Churches?

Can the reluctance of these groups to accept central authority be attributed to

historical forms of Christianity or are there social determinants?
In the early 1980s it was a forbidden subject to talk about the divisions inside the Church, be it Catholic or Protestant. To do so would be considered an 'unfriendly' gesture, and worse, a divisive tactic introduced from the outside. As a result the divisions were not recognized as such and practically no objective study of the situation was done.
This explains partly the poverty of our knowledge about Christianity in China today. On the other hand the study of Christianity in China has too often been done from only an ecclesiological or missiological point of view. Christianity as a social reality cannot become a feasible object of study until empirical data can be gathered without the theological trappings.
Our knowledge about Christianity in China remains fragmentary. We are still far from understanding the patterns of its development, the laws governing its expansion, the underlying issues which make reconciliation difficult. More research, with the cooperation of social sciences, will be necessary before a more coherent picture will emerge both for our own understanding and for relations with Christians in China.

Postscript

Since the paper was written a number of important developments have taken place in China. A general tightening up, already discernible after June 4, is now evident. The Gulf War and especially the collapse of Marxist regimes in Eastern Europe have greatly influenced Chinese thinking on the role of religions in society. Religious leaders from both Protestant Christianity and from Buddhist circles have openly criticized the change in the implementation of government policy. A national conference of government cadres involved in religious work held in December 1990 did not seem to have changed the situation.
As for the Catholic Church, the subject of our paper, the situation has become worse. A clandestine Bishops' Conference, held in November 1989, in opposition to the official Catholic Church has contributed to a hardening of attitudes. In October 1990 the government has taken a less tolerant attitude towards the bishops who have secretly reconciled with the Vatican. There are reports of arrests, closing down of seminaries, etc.
Reports coming from China in 1990 confirm that divisions within the Catholic community continue although the Vatican has taken appropriate measures to stop the uncontrolled consecration of underground bishops. It is still a long way before any real reconciliation can take place.

– excellent article, with core its revelation of new aggressive underground church. Illegible [illegible] lack of "traditional" link, it's most new data of any essay in the book?

6. CHINESE YOUTH TODAY: THE CRISIS OF BELIEF

Feng Chongyi and Gregor Benton

What do Chinese youth today believe? Some people call them the 'thinking generation' on account of their commitment to the search for truth in science, society, and human affairs. Others call them the 'collapsed' or 'lost' generation: a generation that lacks ideals, personal integrity, altruism, selflessness. Still others call them the 'playful' or 'leisure' generation: people who wear outlandish clothes on the street, or who form up on the campus into a 'mahjong faction' and a 'dancing faction'.

'Generational' research is a relatively new branch of sociology in China, and researchers often use the word 'generation' imprecisely. The first person to attempt a systematic analysis in terms of 'generations' was Li Zehou, writing in 1978[1].

Li Zehou divided China's contemporary[2] intelligentsia into six generations. The first was the generation of 1911, which embraced aspects of modern European thought (though not all achieved the same degree of depth in it) and hatched schemes to modernize the Chinese state. Their cultural contribution to China's modern development was great, but their new thinking was shallowly based and easily shaken. The second was the generation of May Fourth (1919), which set out to destroy the Confucian tradition and to create a Chinese Enlightenment; but they were better at bulldozing old structures than at erecting new ones. The third was the generation of the 'Great Revolution' of the 1920s, baptized by the Enlighteners and destined to break the mould of old China and set a pattern for the century: in politics, in science and technology, in philosophy, in history, and in literature. The fourth was the '38 generation', called after a sort of rifle and referring to the generation of Chinese intellectuals who became active in society and politics at the time of the Anti-Japanese War of Resistance, a generation that lacked creativity but diligently elaborated on the pattern set for it a decade earlier. The fifth was the 'liberated generation', whose members took up their positions in society in the late 1940s and the 1950s. They were the generation that 'followed in the mould': ardent and sincere, but intellectually rigid, docile and pious, wholly lacking in creative power. The sixth was the 'generation of Red Guards': a bridge between past and future, who made up in courage and creative spirit for the shortcomings of the generation that had preceded them,

1. Li Zehou, *Zhongguo jindai sixiang shilun* ('A Draft History of Modern Chinese Thought'), Beijing: Renmin chubanshe, 1979, first edn. , pp. 470-471.
2. Usually Chinese define as 'contemporary' Chinese history since 1919, though Li uses the term more loosely.

but who were jolted awake by political betrayal, for once their movement had served its narrow purpose it was ruthlessly suppressed by the same people who with all sorts of libertarian rhetoric had conjured it into being. Unfortunately Li Zehou's portrait of these six generations of Chinese is executed only in broad strokes. In a subsequent book he tried to supplement his characterizations, for example by pointing to some of the weaknesses – cynicism, utilitarianism – as well as the strengths of the 'generation of Red Guards', but still he excused himself for 'not having had the chance' to develop his study in more detail[3].'

Li Zehou's criterion for dividing the human flow into discrete generations is political. He aims to "identify a collective identity for a group of intellectuals affected similarly by certain key, transforming historical events (political events in modern China)". The six generations he identifies "have their distinct fates, path, experience, struggles, ideals, happiness and sorrows[4]".

Recently a young scholar called Liu Xiaofeng proposed a different approach to the problem of generational research. Using notions such as 'biological rhythm' and 'intellectual model' derived from the sociology of knowledge, he identified four generations of intellectuals in contemporary Chinese history. The 'May Fourth generation', born or raised around the turn of the century, took up social and cultural roles between the 1920s and the 1940s. The 'liberated generation', born or raised in the 1930s and early 1940s, entered society in the 1950s and the 1960s. The 'generation of April Fifth[5]', born or raised in the 1940s and early 1950s, took up social and cultural roles in the 1970s and 1980s. And the 'playful generation', born or raised in the 1960s and the 1970s, is now taking up social and cultural roles and will continue to do so into the next century[6].

So it is necessary to distinguish in the present generation between those who grew to maturity in the Cultural Revolution and those who have done so in Deng Xiaoping's so-called 'new era'. The former belong to the thinking generation, the latter to the playful generation. The generation of the Cultural Revolution are brave critics but they want mental supports for their belief, and they think seriously about the past, the present, and the future; whereas the generation of the new era tends toward nihilism or the uncritical embrace of anything that is new, and has eyes only for today.

Obviously, the historian or sociologist's idea of generation is not the same as the biologist's: some old people have young opinions, some young people have old ones. What's more, members of the generation of the Cultural Revolution and of the generation of the new era have much in common, particularly their wish –

3. Li Zehou, *Zhongguo xiandai sixiang shilun* ('A Draft History of Contemporary Chinese Thought'), Beijing: Dongfang chubanshe, 1987, p. 343.
4. Li Zehou and Vera Schwarcz, 'Six Generations of Modern Chinese Intellectuals', *Chinese Studies in History*, vol 17 no. 2.
5. On April 5, 1976, tens of thousands of young people gathered in Tian'anmen Square to mourn Zhou Enlai, leading to an incident that precipitated the fall of the 'Gang of Four'.
6. Liu Xiaofeng, 'Guanyu 'siwu' yidaide shehuixue sikao liji' ('Notes on the Sociology of the 'April Fifth' Generation"), *Dushu*, 1989: 5.

which distinguishes them from the generation of their fathers – to keep abreast of new developments in a changing world. The differences between them are far smaller than the differences between either one of them and the liberated generation.

If literature is the mirror of a nation's soul, we can look in it – especially the literature that treats social issues – for a reflection of the spiritual state of Chinese young people[7] now. After the 'ten years of chaos and catastrophe', Chinese of all classes and ages spat out their bitterness, but the most moving accounts of suffering and disappointment were by intellectual youth. China's 'scarred literature' of the late 1970s took its name from a short story called 'Scar' by Lu Xinhua[8], based on the experiences of intellectual youth. Liu Xinwu's 'Class Director'[9] and 'Awake, Little Brother'[10], Chen Guokai's 'What Should I Do?'[11], Kong Jiesheng's 'The Other Side of the Stream'[12], and Zhang Kangkang's 'Thin Morning Mist'[13] all dissect from various angles the trauma of and the cruel deception practised on intellectual youth in the Cultural Revolution, together with their subsequent indignation, grief, and self-mockery.

The experience had of course been deeply disillusioning. Their heroes had been unmasked as villains, their cause had turned into a nightmare. 'Scarred literature' mapped out the mental and spiritual route that they had followed: their childlike faith in Marx and Mao, their enthusiasm and idealism, their total commitment to 'revolutionary practice', their contempt for the class enemy, their willingness to 'go down to the villages, migrate to the remote borders, climb the high mountains, and live wherever the fatherland requires'[14]. But its end destination turned out to be the fall of the Maoist leaders, the virtual collapse of Chinese society and economy, the restoration to power of the 'capitalist roaders', and the wholesale negation of the Cultural Revolution in which they had played the role of shock-troops. By the late 1970s many of Mao's Red Guards felt that they had lost everything: their youth, their security, their chance to find love, and their chance to study: in return they had been painted by society as the villains of the 'ten years' terror'. History, it seemed, was mocking them: not surprisingly, they mocked back.

7. In China the word 'young' has a rather elastic meaning, but broadly speaking it refers to people under forty. Needless to say, our generalizations about Chinese young people have their limits. What is true of book-trained or 'intellectual' youth is not in all respects true of uneducated youth in China. However, because of their sensitivity to and knowledge of society, young intellectuals in many ways represent the mood of Chinese youth – especially urban youth – as a whole. Is there a difference in the character of youth from one region of China to the next? Yes, there is. Young people in Beijing are more politizised than, say, young people in the great commercial centres of Guangzhou and Shanghai, who are more likely to be 'money-mad'. Even so, these regional differences do not cancel out the basic national identity of Chinese urban youth.
8. Lu Xinhua, 'Shanghen' ('Scar'), *Wenhuibao* (Shanghai), August 11, 1978.
9. Liu Xinwu, 'Ban zhuren' ('Class Director'), *Renmin wenxue* 1977: 11.
10. Liu Xinwu, 'Xinglai ba didi' ('Awake Little Brother'), *Zhongguo qingnian* 1978: 2.
11. Chen Guokui, 'Wo gai zenmo ban?' ('What Should I Do?'), *Zuopin* 1977: 2.
12. Kong Jiesheng, 'Zai xiao he neibian' ('The Other Side of the Stream'), *Zuopin* 1979: 3.
13. Zhang Kangkang, 'Dandande chenwu' ('Thin Morning Mist'), *Shouhuo* 1980: 3.
14. These were the sort of demands made by Chinese Communist leaders on Chinese young people during the Cultural Revolution.

Having grown up in an 'ideologically unified environment', they experienced as unbearably painful the sudden loss of faith. How to evaluate the social role of China's 'unified ideology'? Though Marxism has more to do with science than with soul, Communist ideals were gradually transformed starting with the Russian Revolution into quasi-religious dogmas to support the state, and the Party into a parody of a church with its holy places, martyrs, rituals, feast-days, classics, exegetes, and of course dissenters and heretics. The liberated generation were moulded into the purest embodiment of this religious-style fervour. They willingly subjected themselves to a life of constant toil and criticism, and they loyally put up with the monotony of everyday living under the Party. They outdid even the Puritans in ascetic self-denial. They became receptacles or tools of the Party. The Party in its turn viewed its 'unified ideology' as something sacred and inviolable that can only be incarnated and blindly followed but never criticized, discussed, selectively developed, selectively discarded. So people of this generation lost the capacity for independent thought, and became the 'cogs and rivets' beloved of Maoist ideologues, or sacrificial objects to be crushed beneath the Party juggernaut. Whatever dissatisfaction they dared feel, they could express only in terms of passive scepticism. Naturally there were exceptions, for example Li Zehou, whom young Chinese today honour and respect as a profound and daring thinker. And though their unthinking, unswerving loyalty belongs to what Liu Binyan, one of China's veteran left-wing dissenters, would call the first rather than the second kind[15], it is still hard not to admire the public spirit of the liberated generation. But even though they had no 'evil in their hearts', the outcome of the political system they helped bring into being harmed China greatly.
There is a wide gulf between the liberated generation and the generation of the Cultural Revolution. This latter generation, unlike the former, was not completely assimilated to Stalinist norms of political behaviour. Never having been plucked from the floods and flames by the Party, they felt less need than their 'liberated' predecessors to bow down before its leaders. During the Cultural Revolution their thinking did not proceed entirely along predetermined paths. They had some leeway for experimentation and debate. Though today their movement is associated almost exclusively with violence and terror, it began as a movement against privilege and corruption, inspired by the ideal of national self-reliance, and it taught millions of young Chinese self-discipline, self-organization, and the duty to contest the immoral exercise of power. At the end of the nightmare they were not afraid to accuse those who had cruelly deceived and harmed them, and many of them hoped to rediscover and remould themselves and to find new ideals by which to shape society.
Since the core ideology of the contemporary Chinese state is a modern superstition that thrives on closed and damaged minds, those who live under it cannot easily find the way to a satisfactory truth. As is the way with religions in decay, the first product of the dissolution of this rigid ideological system was intel

15. Liu Binyan, 'Dierzhong zhongcheng' ('The Second Kind of Loyalty'), in *Liu Binyan baogao wenxue*, Hongkong: Minchuang chubanshe, 1987.

lectual chaos. After 1976 large numbers of people in China lost all faith and belief. "When you think falsehood is truth," wrote Cao Xueqin, author of the classic eighteenth-century novel *Dream of the Red Chamber* "then truth is falsehood. When you believe nothing to be something, then something is nothing." The generation of Red Guards originally believed unconditionally in Marxism-Leninism and Mao Zedong Thought: they were confident that they could 'win a hundred victories in a hundred battles'. But instead they plunged China and themselves into tragedy, so their faith collapsed and they felt that as a generation they had been squeezed dry and tossed away. There is a parallel here with the generation of May Fourth. Around the turn of the century the Confucian value system in which that generation had been trained collapsed together with the Qing and (later) Yuan Shikai, so its members had to look for new ways of restoring health and strength to China. But the international setting in 1919 was quite different from what it is today, and after the Confucian collapse radical youth found their way comparatively quickly to the 'democracy and science' through which the West had apparently grown strong, and in particular to 'Marxism', which in Russia seemed at the time to have brought new life to the Russian nation, justice to its international relations, and liberation to its common people. But members of the generation of the Cultural Revolution faced a special difficulty: the 'Marxism' to which they owed allegiance had proved to be a bringer of bad times, so they lost faith in it. Yet these young people were not minded either to 'lean' in the opposite direction by collectively embracing any of the other isms currently being imported from the West. So after the winding up of the Cultural Revolution they waged intellectual guerrilla warfare, snatching eclectically and piecemeal at ideas of all kinds but never developing any of them in a systematic way. As a reaction to abstract collectivism of the sort that negates human individuality, some of them promoted the idea of 'free competition' under the standard of extreme individualism[16]. Others, alienated by the constant tension of political struggle and campaigns, sought solace in religion and the freeing of the spirit[17]. Still others looked to sexual love as a refuge and fulfilment[18]. Existentialism and 'free choice' flourished in some quarters; some young Chinese reacted against the vulgar enslavements of society by promoting a cult of the Nietzschean superman. And of course no few people tried to find their way to the true, original form of Marxism by combing the writings of Marx, where they discovered dangerous concepts like humanism and alienation[19].

If the special quality of today's generation is thinking, its members naturally welcomed China's 'second liberation' in 1979, but still obstacles stand between them and the truth. Their strength lies in their optimism and ardour. Even so,

16. Zhang Xinxin, 'Zai tongyi diping xianshang' ('On the Same Horizon'), *Shouhuo*, 1981: 6.
17. Li Ping, 'Wanxia xiaoshi de shihou' ('When Dusk Disappeared'), *Shiyue* 1981: 1.
18. Zhang Jie, 'Ai shi buneng wangjide' ('Love, Something That Cannot Be Forgotten'), *Beijing wenyi*, 1979: 11.
19. Wang Ruoshui, *Wei rendaozhuyi bianhu*, ('In Defence of Humanism'), Beijing: Sanlian shudian, 1986. Wang Ruoshui is in his sixties, but most members of the group of Marxist humanists are young people.

many of the generation of the Cultural Revolution are considered in China to have fallen beyond redemption. After the original collapse of faith many of them could find no new supports, nor did they seek any. They even abominated thought itself, and sank into mindless pessimism. At first some hoped that they might discover something of value in life; finding nothing, they gave up the search[20]. Others thought that the best thing was to give up the tedium of politics and society and retreat instead into family life, but all they found there was more tedium[21]. What both these attitudes have in common is cynicism.
But for all its cynicism, the generation of the Cultural Revolution is also capable of a form of idealism – often heavily sentimental, but still idealism – founded in concepts like equality, sincerity, and justice recalled from their childhood. Members of the playful generation, on the other hand, tend toward true nihilism. If they believe in anything, it is nothing. They have developed to its extreme the cynicism that characterizes part of the generation of the Cultural Revolution. They ridicule the old Maoist moral preaching, with its Lei Fengs and other selfless toilers for the common good created by the official propaganda machine[22]. They hate wooden conformity and society's plethora of rules and regulations, which they do their best to thwart and subvert[23]. They neglect themselves, they burst out crying for no reason, they burst out laughing for no reason, they scream and shout; life, love, work – these are a game with no rules; only that which is 'new' and 'strange' can turn them on, and in some cases even that cannot.[24] They are contemptuous of old forms of fame, achievement, morality, status, and authority, but they also scorn the unscrupulous manoeuvring and enslavement to cash and vulgarity that in their view characterizes Chinese society now. In short, 'everything is bloody boring[25]'. If poetry is the antenna of the soul, then through the 'rising poets' who in recent years have invaded China's literary forum we can also trace the intellectual orbit of Chinese youth today. A few years ago a group known as the 'obscure poets' presented themselves as the mouthpiece of the generation of the Cultural Revolution. Their poetry is ambiguous in form, conception, and execution, its shape and rhythm changes in a seemingly random way, the sentiments it voices are mobile and ethereal. Many people reproach these poets for writing in a mode that deliberately defies comprehension, but the style that they adopt successfully conveys their strong antipathy to obscurantist dogmas and social vices, together with their pursuit of a new but as yet unapprehended ideal society. They shout battle-cries or ice-cold denunciations,[27] they give faint voice to their deep dis-

20. Dong Huiping, 'Xunzhao' ('Searching'), *Qingchun* 1980: 2.
21. Zhang Xinxin, 'Women zhege nianjide meng' ('The Dream of Our Age'), *Shouhuo* 1980: 4.
22. Tan Li, 'Yige xingqiliude wanshang' ('One Saturday Evening'), *Qingnian zuojia* 1981, inaugural edition.
23. Xu Jun, 'Jinde yun' ('Near Clouds'), *Sichuan wenxue* 1982: 1.
24. Liu Suola, *Ni bie wu xuanze* ('You Have No Other Choice'), Beijing: Zuojia chubanshe, 1986.
25. Chen Jiangong, 'Maomao' ('Long Hair'), *Shiyue* 1986: 2.
26. Xu Xing, 'Wu zhuti bianzou' ('Variations without a Theme'), *Renmin wenxue* 1985: 7.
27. Bei Dao, 'Huida' ('Answer') and 'Yu ye' ('Rainy Night'), in Yan Yuejun, (ed.), *Menglong shixuan* ('An Anthology of Obscure Poetry'), Shenyang: Chunfeng wenyi chubanshe, 1985, pp. 1-2 and 13-14.

tress,[28] they express their worries about the present and the future.[29] Although their writing is in the main ambiguous, they always clearly distinguish between right and wrong. The 'experimental poets' who succeeded them and can be considered as representatives of the playful generation have a quite different approach to their art, which they pursue like a bizarre game of words or an assemblage of irrational and abstract symbols, without ever venturing serious statements about values.[30] "That man is mad," writes a typical representative of this school, "and after death he will get madder still; you're playing with the bottom of a china cup, but just because he's mad you cannot call him mad."[31]

Even popular songs can accurately reflect the mind of contemporary Chinese youth. The tender and melancholy "Southeastern style" (based on the popular music of Hong Kong and Taiwan) that became so popular throughout China in the late 1970s and the early 1980s strikingly matched the mood of the generation of the Cultural Revolution: their emotional exhaustion, their urgent need for consolation, the melancholy and restrained accusations that they flung at society and the powers that be. This Southeastern style of popular music was closely followed by the Northwestern style, which also strongly reflects the changing mood of that generation of Chinese youth. Its throbbing pulse symbolizes their wish to act, but the singer's raucous screaming expresses their sense of grief and powerlessness. By the time that Cui Jian's 'Yiwu suoyou' ('I have nothing') came onto the Chinese music market, the playful generation had already come into its own. Cui Jian articulated the sense of emptiness of those who know that they are oppressed but can find no way out of their predicament. "Why does your hand tremble? Why do your tears flow? Is it becauce I own nothing that you say you love me?"

In short, some members of the generation of the Cultural Revolution and most members of the playful generation adopt an attitude of indifference toward important issues of morality and belief. Even so, compared with the cheap idcalism, shallow optimism, and abject docility of the liberated generation, their scepticism, confusion, and dissatisfaction is still a sort of progress. Only in the wake of the catastrophe born of the rule of modern superstition and ossified belief can we really appreciate the true value of doubt and self-doubt. For doubt, and even 'decadence', are the negation of superstition; and that negation is itself a precondition for China's further progress. It allows people coolly and rationally to ponder their present dilemma and the path from it. In China there is a saying: 'There is nothing sadder than the death of heart.' Passive resistance to irrational power is better than accommodation to it. That's why Wang Meng, a veteran writer with excellent credentials in the struggle against political vice,

28. Shu Ting, 'Zhubei – dahaide yanlei' ('Mother-of-Pearl: Tear of the Sea') and 'Yubie' (Farewell in the Rain'), in Yan Yuejun, (ed.), op. cit., pp. 44-45 and 58.
29. Gu Cheng, 'Anjian' ('Case') and 'Zuotian, xiang heisede she' ('Yesterday, Like a Black Snake'), in Yan Yuejun, (ed.), op. cit., pp. 117 and 136.
30. Tang Xiaodu and Wang Jiaxin, (eds.), *Zhongguo dangdai shiyan shixuan* ('An Anthology of Contemporary Experimental Poetry'), Shenyang: Chunfeng wenyi chubanshe, 1987.
31. Lu Yimin, 'Ni xing zai qingchen' ('You Wake in the Early Morning'), in Tang Xiaodu and Wang Jiaxin, (eds.), op. cit., p. 77.

said of the present generation: "Under an outer garment of play-acting and self-raillery they have discovered the chaotic but moving voice of youth."[32] Even so, their cynicism and despair, their 'three crises of belief' (crisis of faith, crisis of confidence, crisis of trust), and their retreat into egoism are facts that cannot be disregarded.[33]

Whence this cynicism and despair? The official explanation is that China's youth today has been 'spiritually polluted' by the West. On the surface there would seem to be some truth in this. After all, many young Chinese are said to worship the West, and the 'bad habits' that they have developed over the last few years are far more visible and widespread in Western countries than they are in China. But Deng Xiaoping's ideologues should not forget that according to central tenets of their own interpretation of 'dialectical materialism', the 'internal factor' is invariably decisive. Why in East-West intercourse did China not 'pollute' the West instead of vice versa (as it started to do for a brief moment in 1968, when Western student radicals still entertained a romantic view of the Cultural Revolution)? How after decades of 'meticulous attention to the nurturing' of the spirit of Chinese youth by the Party could that same spirit be hijacked overnight by foreigners? Actually, today's infatuation with the West is not the cause but the effect of this despair. Another 'theory' current in China is that some young Chinese willingly corrupt and debase themselves, because as children and grandchildren of the revolution they have grown up spoiled and pampered. But the idea is quite superficial. If we want to know why Chinese young people regularly 'abase' themselves, we should look less in their heads and more to the nature of present-day Chinese society.

For the sickness that infects the spirit of Chinese youth is the reflection of a general sickness in Chinese society as a whole. Young people are not the only ones, but they are more vulnerable to the malaise, for they are more sensitive to the social mood. In a word, this sickness is a product of a general social crisis: of the three crises of belief and of the hedonistic, *fin de siècle* frenzy that now grips China. Its roots lie in the system of Stalinist rule, the inability of China's ruling group to point a way out for the country, and the rampant spread of commodity capitalism throughout the economy.

It would be unfair to say that the Chinese Communist Party only knows how to destroy things and not how to build them. After 1949 China became an independent and united nation, with the beginnings of an industrial base and a roused populace. But unfortunately the foundations on which the leaders of the Party constructed this new China were copied from Soviet Stalinism. The regime that the Communist leaders established in 1949 monopolized political decision, even

32. Wang Meng, 'Xu' ('Introduction') to Liu Suola, *Ni bie wu xuanze*.

33. Some people say that since 1949 Chinese morals have developed according to the following pattern: 'In the 1950s people helped one another, in the 1960s they rectified one another, in the 1970s they struggled against one another, in the 1980s each looks after himself'. The question is, is there not a relationship between the various stages in this sequence, and has not the one paved the way to the next? For example, by 'denying self' the liberated generation in the long run destroyed the basis for true collectivism and so paved the way for a Hobbesian war of all against all.

against the classes they claimed to represent. They had long been used in the villages to seeing themselves as the sole fount of wisdom, authority, honours, and reward. Politically, liberation roused great expectations in the Chinese people, but power under the new system – an amalgam of traditional and modern autocracy, foreign and homegrown – gravitated into the hands of government officials, with the 'masses' cast in the humble role of 'servants of the state'. The new system oppressed and infantilized the people, and destroyed their creative powers. At the same time, it further corrupted the new officialdom, which controlled power both political and economic and was unaccountable and unrepresentative. The way to get ahead under this system is to abase yourself and concur with everything that your superiors tell you, so it is the complete reverse of 'natural selection', for it selects those least suited to the competent and responsible exercise of power in society. All economic life becomes subject to the wishes, desires, and interests of the state, i.e. of officialdom. So ordinary citizens lose their enthusiasm for work and start 'going slow'. This then is the crux of the terminal sickness of Chinese economy. But the system's crowning shame is its destruction of cultural and intellectual life. The Stalinist state cleverly reduces Marxism to a set of religious-style ritualistic formulas with which to defend its own privileges and control the people. In so doing, it deals a fatal blow to the reputation of Marxism and effectively outlaws creative thougt. Under this political, economic, and cultural system, many people – especially young people – inevitably become depressed in spirit and (as a mute expression of resentment) turn violently against all forms of political preaching, political ideals, and even politics itself. They go out of their way to shock society by violating its morality and mores.

Such a system infects with sickness the entire fabric of society, which is why China's 'socialist' state (and not only China's) was forced to set out on the road to reform. Within ten short years the changes had greatly enlivened China's villages and cities. Chinese young people threw themselves into the reforms with gusto, just like youngsters of an earlier age had thrown themselves into the Cultural Revolution. But because the 'grand designer' Deng Xiaoping is not prepared to challenge the entrenched power of the Party that he leads, he is unable to meet the expectations that he himself has raised. Where political as opposed to economic reform is concerned, he merely tinkers with the existing system, and so he must dash the hopes of the constituency he has created. What he cannot do is frankly admit the failure of his project and encourage the emergence of a social system in which people cooperate and develop their creative powers to the full under conditions of democracy. Deng Xiaoping has no intention of allowing China to open fully to the world on many fronts, so that Chinese people can renew their damaged culture by absorbing the fruits of all human civilization. According to Deng's 'grand design', even by the middle of the next century China will still be poor in international terms. So people feel cheated and disappointed. Deng Xiaoping's real cake is less capable of inspiring enthusiasm than Mao's painted one. As for Deng's 'socialism with Chinese features', it appears in practice to be little more than a mixture of Stalinist politics and capitalist economics, garnished with a dash of Chinese 'feudal' ideology.

This then is the real explanation of the trend toward pessimistic despair and sagging morale among today's young people, who find few channels through which to develop their abilities.

We should not forget that there is an important link between the abnormal state of mind of China's youth and the current economic reforms. Where the Chinese authorities do not blame this spiritual malaise on foreign pollution or lack of self-respect, they blame it on the Cultural Revolution and explain it as an overreaction to the crimes of Lin Biao and the 'Gang of Four'. In this way they avoid inculpating their own leadership and policies. But the Chinese public is increasingly unprepared to accept events that happened in the 1960s and the 1970s as an explanation for the crisis of the 1980s.

What of the mood of youth under the reforms? Many young people expected reform to smash the system of 'ownership by officialdom' and put power and productive resources back into the hands of the people, who could then begin to play an active role as 'masters of society' and invest their energy in developing the economy. To a certain extent, the reforms have been successful. But because a 'market economy' has been grafted onto a bureaucratic state, the original 'bureaucratic economy' has crossed with the 'market mechanism' to produce a class of 'money-bags', 'official speculators', and 'cadre princes' in the Party who use their political power to 'get rich first' in the new two-track economy. So it's not surprising that the rest of society looks to earn cash wherever and however it can, and the devil take the hindmost. Under these circumstances the 'commodity economy' is a Pandora's box of egoism, greed, sycophancy, deceit, violence, crime, graft, gambling, prostitution, and all the other evils that infest Chinese society today. In a few respects the situation is even worse than in the West during the period of primitieve accumulation of capital. When reform was first mooted, well-meaning intellectuals believed that it was the key to overcoming privilege, that commodities and cash would equalize Chinese society. But a commodity economy grafted onto an existing system of privilege simply compounds the privilege and allows it to run rampant. The shameless quest for riches seemed at some points to have driven the whole of China mad. It was as the novelist Jia Ping'ao described: nervous anxiety has become China's overriding national characteristic.[34] And of course it is young people who are the most nervous and the most anxious.

Since China's political system is the source of China's troubles, it is quite absurd to think (as some people in the Chinese Government apparently do) that the way out of the present crisis is to fight to restore 'belief' in Stalinist politics. 'Thought reform' will not solve a problem that has its roots not in thought but in material life and social relations. The best cure for China's crisis of the spirit is a movement to change society and bury Stalinism. Only radical social change can restore faith to China's youth and enthuse them to play a constructive role in society. The pity is that Stalinism everywhere has done enormous harm to the socialist cause. Chinese people say that 'it's easy to dodge a spear thrown in the open, but hard to dodge one thrown from hiding'. Socialism's public enemies

34. Jia Ping'ao, 'Fuzao' ('Nervous Anxiety'), *Shouhuo* 1987: 1.

are less dangerous than its hidden ones, who launch their attacks under the Red Flag. So there's a danger of burying socialism along with Stalinism in China. In that case the best chance of a resurrection would lie with China's critical youth, whose new explorations in democracy and socialism deserve support. They are today putting into practice the ideals of the first generation of Chinese Marxists: they are fighting to heal the 'sequelae of the revolution', and to reverse the alienation of power by creating a society based on freedom, equality, peace, democracy, and prosperity.

Skip for review

7. TRAIN UP A CHILD: ATTITUDES TOWARDS RELIGION AND ATHEISM AMONG CHINESE STUDENTS (Survey in U.K.)

Alan Hunter and Don Rimmington

Introduction

"Train up a child in the way he should go: and when he is old he will not depart from it": already in the Bible (Proverbs 22:6) we find reference to what is now called social conditioning. Adherence to religious organizations can be reasonably well predicted for a given population when we know social background, education and parents' beliefs. But one should avoid simplistic determinism. At times a new religious orientation may arise, or old ideas revive, with unpredictable consequences: human life is grounded in material circumstances, but the response of the human spirit can be unexpected, colourful in its variety. Since 1949 the Chinese state and its education system has been resolutely atheist; the question addressed in this paper is to what extent this has trained up a generation of non-believers.

Claims have been made concerning a recent revival of religion in China, among both rural and urban populations, including university students. On anecdotal evidence, some students at least, presumably disillusioned with Marxism, expressed considerable interest in religion in the 1980s. We heard that the short story "When Dusk Disappeared[1]" for example, which is perhaps the only contemporary literary work from the PRC to deal seriously and extensively with religious questions, was earnestly transcribed and passed from hand to hand as samizdat before publication. We read reports that churches in Beijing and Shanghai were sometimes packed with young people. The growth of interest was also admitted by a team of Chinese social scientists[2]. Since there are a relatively large number of Chinese students in Britain, it appeared feasible to conduct an empirical study, by means of a postal survey, to test these claims. The survey was conducted in November and December 1989 from the Department of East Asian Studies, Leeds University.

The Questionnaire And Respondents

The questionnaire (summarized here as the Appendix) asks for yes/no answers and modified Likert scale responses, and requests written information on par-

1. Li Ping (pseudonym) "Wanxia xiaoshi de shihou" (When Dusk Disappeared), *Shiyue*, 1981 No.1, pp. 77-134.
2. Xiao Zhitian, "Some Opinions on Present Religious Phenomena", *Ching Feng*, Vol 26 No. 4, December 1983.

ticular topics[3]. The three parts of the questionnaire cover demographic details and two longer sections on religion: 'general attitude' and 'personal experience'. General attitude concerns the religions that exist in China, level of interest in existential questions, and attitudes towards life after death, petitionary prayer and fortune-telling. Most of these questions were adapted from other questionnaires. The question on fortune telling was included because of the prevalence of this activity in Chinese society, including in the PRC in the 1980s[4]. Personal experience asks for information about education, influences and personal spiritual experience. The key question "Have you ever felt you were in close contact with something holy?" (with some variety of phrasing) has been a standard feature in several major studies. Other questions were adapted from a survey of quasi-religious experiences among British young people[5].

The questionnaire left spaces where respondents were asked to volunteer information in an open-ended way. 'General attitude' requested comments concerning life after death, prayer and fortune telling. In 'Personal experience' we received more extensive personal thoughts concerning religious experience and education. Most of the comments were relatively short – a few lines on average – although some respondents took the trouble to reply at length. Respondents were invited to write in Chinese if they wished. Few did so and the level of English in the answers was high enough to suggest that they had had little difficulty in coping with the linguistic aspects of the questionnaire as a whole: answers were almost all clear and to the point. The cumulative information from these replies allowed a more subtle analysis of the statistical information.

A secondary aim of the study was to compare our findings with those from other surveys. Surveys on religion have been conducted on western populations, but they would not be suitable for Chinese people who had received little or no formal religious teaching and for whom factors such as church attendance would be largely irrelevant. It would have been desirable simply to use an existing questionnaire, as this would have allowed direct comparisons between our Chinese population and others, e.g the Canadians studied by Bibby or the 'foreign students' from many nations studied by Yinger[6]. This was inadvisable for two main reasons. In the first place, other questionnaires seemed to assume that religious belief would be widespread among respondents. They offered little space for atheists or agnostics to express thoughts about religion other than stat-

3. The questionnaire was designed after detailed consultation with Dr C. Perring, a research psychologist, and Mr P.D. Constable, a statistician with survey experience, to both of whom we are most grateful.
4. See for example Gong Jianlong, "Why are superstitious activities on the rise again?", in David S.K. Chu (ed.), *Sociology and Society in Contemporary China, 1979-83*, New York: M.E. Sharpe, 1983, pp. 204-11.
5. M. Paffard, *Inglorious Wordsworths: A Study of Some Transcendent Experiences in Childhood and Adolescence*, London: Hodder and Stoughton, 1973.
6. R.W. Bibby, "Religion and Modernity: The Canadian Case", *Journal for the Scientific Study of Religion*, Vol 18 No 1, 1979, pp. 1-17. R.W. Bibby, "Searching for Invisible Threads: Meaning Systems in Contemporary Canada", *Journal for the Scientific Study of Religion*, Vol 22 No 2, 1983, pp. 101-119. J-M. Yinger, "A Comparative Study of the Substructures of Religion", *Journal for the Scientific Study of Religion*, Vol 16 No 1, 1977, pp. 67-86.

ing non-belief. Some of our respondents object strongly to religion and they would only be able to express this if the the questionnaire were suitably designed. Secondly, most surveys relate largely if not exclusively to Christianity. This would clearly be unsuitable for Chinese people. We anticipated that some students might have an interest in Christianity, but not in a way that would be directly comparable to people raised in a Christian or 'post-Christian' culture. Recognising that comparisons would be limited, we decided to retain questions from existing surveys on a selective basis.

405 questionnaires together with an explanatory letter requesting co-operation were distributed with the kind assistance of registrar's offices in six British universities. Respondents were offered a brief synopsis of findings, and assured that all data would be treated confidentially and anonymously. 120 replies were received, all of which were well completed. Three were not included since the respondents had had at least some schooling in Taiwan or Hong Kong. We believe all others were educated entirely in the PRC until they arrived in Britain for study. Five replies arrived too late to be used. A response rate of 40 - 50% is considered good for a postal survey in psychology and we were pleased with our response rate of ca. 30%, having anticipated that two factors might work against it: language difficulties and possible anxiety about disapproval from Chinese authorities. In the event, the response rate suggests that these did not play an undue role.

This survey, like others of its kind, must be treated with some reservations, which are perhaps worth spelling out here. In the first place, we cannot assume complete accuracy. Some respondents may have had language difficulties. Others may have adopted the 'good respondent' syndrome, i.e. unconsciously wished to provide answers they assumed we wished to read. Others may have been reluctant to write anything contrary to officially approved attitudes. Second, respondents formed ca. 30% of recipients of our questionnaire and are thus a self-selecting group. This is normal with such surveys, but it does leave open the question as to how their views might differ from the remaining 70%. Third, Chinese students abroad form a tiny percentage of Chinese students in general. We could anticipate various distorting factors: more foreign contact than average, higher success in examinations, a greater proportion of natural scientists and males. Nevertheless the unique nature of this exploratory study warrants reporting.

Survey Data

Valid responses received were 112 out of 405 forms distributed. Approximately 70 respondents contributed comments ranging from a few words to a few hundred. The data were analyzed on the SPSSX program which is widely used in the social sciences. They were tested for statistical significance (Pearson product-moment correlation (r)) and some were found significant at the p .05 level, i.e. there is reason to believe that they are more than chance results. An interesting point, discussed below, is that many findings showed little change when cross-tabulated with the demographic variables. We have reported some results which were not statistically significant at the p .05 level, but which nonetheless may indicate trends which would be worth investigating if more data could be collected.

The demographic data can be briefly summarized (in %, to nearest whole number). Our respondents were 20% female and 80% male. 30% were aged 26 or less; 38% between 27 and 32; and 32% were 32 or older. 20% came from Beijing, 40% from North China and 35% from South China (5% missing). 76% were studying natural sciences, 13% social sciences and 10% humanities (1% missing). 20% had arrived in Britain after April 1989, 41% between January 1988 and April 1989, 37% before January 1988 (2% missing). 52% reported attempts at artistic work and 47% reported none (1% missing).

We feel it is likely that the gender, age, arrival date and main subject of studies ratios reflect the overall ratio among Chinese students in Britain rather than an important difference in response rates. It is interesting to note the large proportion of respondents who give Beijing as their home town - 20% of the sample, while Beijing has ca. 1% of the Chinese population. Shanghai was the next city with 6.5% of respondents. These data suggest that students from Beijing, and to a lesser extent Shanghai, are in a highly advantageous position for study outside China, although it may be that some students moved to Beijing for studies and now regard it as their home town. The division here between North and South China is somewhat arbitrary, the Yangtze being taken as the approximate dividing marker.

Table 1: *Religious belief of parents* (in %, N = 112)

None	46.4
Buddhism	11.6
Christianity	1.8
Other	1.8
Missing	38.4

These data are problematic but interesting, in particular the very large number of missing replies, surpassed only by the question on methods of fortune-telling which was of little relevance to most respondents. We considered various possible reasons for this, e.g. reluctance to ascribe a religion in case of eventual breach of confidentiality, sense of shame if one's parents subscribed to 'feudal superstition', or feeling that the question was badly phrased or irrelevant. A Chinese colleague we interviewed suggested that the most likely reason was that many young people simply did not know what their parents' beliefs were and so could not write anything. He explained that for many years between 1950 and 1978 it was dangerous to practice any form of religion, and many people chose not to discuss the question at all. In those years religion played only a small role in national life and many children might have grown up without any idea of their parents' real beliefs. It is unfortunate that the data are rather limited. One would normally expect parental belief to be very important in determining the religious orientation of children, and we will see that our survey tends to confirm this expectation. It is clearly an area where further research would be useful.

In Part Two, question 8 concerned self-reporting of religious belief. Replies were: committed .9%, curious 53.6%, not religious 40.2, negative 1.8% and other 3.6%. Table 2 shows attitudes to the major religions found in China (question 9):

Table 2: *Attitudes towards various religions* (in %, N = 112)

	Christianity	Buddhism	Islam	Taoism/popular
True	3.6	7.1	0	5.4
Sympathy	35.7	31.1	10.7	25.0
Neutral	48.2	49.1	62.5	50.0
Opposed	3.6	4.5	12.5	7.1
Missing	8.9	8.0	14.3	12.5

Christianity, Buddhism and Taoism/popular religions show a similar profile, while Islam is distinctly less popular. Testing for significance suggested that there is no correlation between this negativity towards Islam and length of stay in Britain, so it seems unlikely that it is a result of the presentation of negative stereotypes in the western media, although of course these may have confirmed an earlier attitude[7].

In response to question 9, three topics - concerning purpose of life, happiness and cause of suffering - elicited a high level of interest, more than 90% of respondents stating that they thought about these questions sometimes or often, and did not consider them a waste of time. It is worth noting that these are issues that might be of interest to religious or non-religious thinkers. Much less interest was expressed in the questions relating to creation and life after death, especially the latter: 60% of respondents said they never thought about it. However when asked about life after death (question 12) there was a good response rate: ca. 10% believed in some form of life after death, 29% were unsure and 53% did not believe (7% 'other' and 1% missing). Belief in reincarnation scored low (2.7%) suggesting confirmation that although this concept was an important element of Buddhist teaching, it never gained the wide popular acceptance in China that it enjoys in India. Only two respondents believed in reward/punishment after death. On the whole it seemed that the question of life after death inspired little interest or belief among our sample.

Respondents were generally sceptical about petitionary prayer and fortune-telling (questions 13-14). In both cases ca. 30% answered 'possible' as opposed to 70% 'very doubtful' or 'no'. Nobody had a firm belief in prayer and only one person in fortune telling. 6.3% mentioned some interest in fengshui and 4.5% in physiognomy but overall there was little response to the second part of question 14 on particular forms of fortune-telling (86% missing). The high number of missing responses is not surprising given the low level of credence accorded to

7. For a brilliant analysis of media stereotypes see E.W. Said, *Covering Islam*, (London: Routledge and Kegan Paul, 1981).

fortune telling by the students in our survey. This scepticism contrasts strongly with the widespread attachment to fortune-telling and petitionary prayer reported in traditional Chinese society. It is presumably related to the high standard of education of our sample.

Table 3: *Contact with something holy or beyond normal consciousness* (in %, N = 112)

Often	2.7
Sometimes	33.9
Never	61.6
Missing	1.8

This is an important question since it has been asked, with slight variation of wording, in many other surveys, from which some comparative data are given in the next section. Around 36% of our sample have experienced some kind of mystical or spiritual feelings which, perhaps surprisingly, coincides well with many findings in the USA and Europe.

Responses to the question on education offered strong confirmation that religions in Chinese schools were presented in a negative way (30%) or not at all (69%) during respondents' school-days (c. 1960-85). A few respondents noted that their parents, even when they were not religious themselves, had expressed a more sympathetic attitude towards religions than school teachers had.

In question 18 respondents were asked to read two short passages, a report of a mystical experience occasioned by contact with nature, and a response to a few words by Mother Teresa of Calcutta. They were then asked if they had had similar experiences themselves and to make any relevant comments. 59% said they had had experiences in some way similar and 30% denied this (11% missing). Of those who felt they had had similar experiences, several expressly stated that they did not interpret these in a religious way but as purely natural phenomena. The passages were included partly to stimulate comments, as was question 19 which simply asked for further thoughts about religion or atheism. As an approximate analysis we counted comments which clearly expressed a scientistic, atheist viewpoint and those which used terms such as 'love', 'freedom' or 'spiritual' in a positive sense:

Table 4: *Comments volunteered on form* (in %, N = 112)

Use of words such as 'freedom, love, spiritual'	18
Tending towards atheism/scientism	22
No comment or hard to classify in these terms	60

Next, on the basis of responses to several different questions, we produced a composite profile that gives an overall assessment of the respondent's religious orientation or disposition. Persons who indicated some form of interest in religious belief (answers 'a' or 'b' to question 8); positive attitude towards particular religions ('true' or 'sympathy' to question 9); interest in existential questions ('often' or 'sometimes' to all question 10); and some personal religious experience ('often' or 'sometimes' to question 15) were coded 'favourable'. Persons who scored negatively on the questions relating to religion ('c' or 'd' to question 8; 'neutral' or 'opposed' to question 9; 'never' to question 15) were coded 'negative'. Other respondents were coded 'neutral'. The result from the survey as a whole was 'favourable' 20.5%, 'negative' 22.5%, 'neutral' 57.0%. This was very close to the result obtained from analysis of comments (see Table 4), and, we believe, an important overall finding of the survey.

We were then able to examine cross-tabulations of this 'general religious orientation' with the demographic variables. The most outstanding feature of this exercise was a striking similarity shown when taking age, gender, home, main subject and date of arrival as variables, almost none of which produced results of statistical significance at the p .05 level. Perhaps the main conclusion to be drawn is that the sample is a surprisingly homogeneous group. Does this sugggest a highly standardized output through the Chinese educational system despite the enormous population and geographic diversity of China? The only significant result here was:

Table 5: *Date of arrival/purpose of life* (N = 104)
(How often do you think of the question 'What is the purpose of life'?)

Arrival	Often	Sometime/never
Since April 89	10	11
Jan 88-April 89	31	12
Before Jan 88	19	21 (r = .04)

There is clearly a peak of interest in this question in about the second year of a student's stay in Britain. Is it perhaps a time for soul-searching and wondering about one's future?

The only other data which even suggested a trend were in the following:

1. Home town/attitude towards Christianity. Respondents from North China are more likely to be neutral or opposed to Christianity than are respondents from Beijing or South China (r = .1). This trend is not observed in other aspects of belief or attitude.
2. Main subject of study/attitude towards Christianity. Social scientists and arts students are more inclined to believe Christianity true or to regard it with sympathy compared to natural scientists (r = .09).

As already mentioned, parents' belief was a particularly interesting variable, producing two significant results and two indications of trends:

Table 6: *Parents' religion/General attitude towards religion*: (N = 65)

	True/sympathy	Neutral/opposed
Parents religion:		
None	24	25
Any	13	3 (r = .02)

Thus, children of parents with some religion are more likely to have a favourable attitude towards religions than children of non-believers. However it is

interesting that they are not more likely to believe in religion themselves, although they are more likely to believe in some kind of life after death (r = .04). There is also a possible trend (r = .11) for children of religious parents to claim contact with something holy or outside normal consciousness more often than others, and the rather strange result that such children are less likely than others to answer 'often' to question 10 a, concerning creation (r = .08).
Finally, attempts at art appear to be related to level of interest in religious or philosophical questions. Those who have done some independent artistic work are much more likely than their non-artistic counterparts to report thinking about the purpose of life (r = .05) and the cause of suffering (r = .02) . There is also a trend (r = .1) for them to be more likely to believe in some form of life after death.

Comparisons With Other Surveys

R.W. Bibby conducted two large surveys in Canada, with about 2,000 and 1,500 respondents respectively[8]. In the 1983 survey, religious self-assessment was: committed 43%, mild interest 25%, not religious 21%, other 11%. Approximately 60% of respondents accepted some major elements of Christian faith, and only 2% were specifically non-religious, i.e. scored negative on all Christian beliefs, had low or no interest in religions and saw themselves as non-religious. There was a high level of belief (90% +) in some form of life after death among all respondents except a handful of 'humanists'. A major American survey produced results of a comparable order for the USA: 47% of respondents said they had made a personal commitment to Christ, and 74% saw themselves as religious believers[9]. This is of course a striking contrast with the Chinese students, of whom only one claimed 'commitment' to religion, and of whom 53% were firm disbelievers in life after death.
Bibby also asked the questions used for our question 10: to what extent do you think about creation, purpose of life, happiness, suffering and life after death? Comparing his answers with the data from our survey, we find that the reported level of interest in these 'existential' questions is on the whole considerably higher among the Chinese students, particularly on the question concerning the purpose of life: 31% of Canadians thought about it 'often' compared with 55% of Chinese. A notable exception was the question on life after death, thought about 'often' by 26% of Canadians but only 4% of Chinese. Two factors may contibute to these results: our sample of students are all highly educated, while the Canadian sample was a cross-section of the population; and our average age was around 30, perhaps too young for death to be a major issue. As we have seen already, the question of life after death does not seem to generate much interest among our respondents.
In Canada, attitudes towards astrology were: firm belief 5%, possible 44%,

8. See note 5 for details.
9. *Conneticut Mutual Life Report on American Values in the 1980s: The Impact of Belief*, New York: Research and Forecasts, Inc., 1981.

very doubtful 33% and firm disbelief 18%. Comparing this with our reports of belief in fortune-telling (firm belief 1%, possible 28%, very doubtful 37% and firm disbelief 29% with 5% missing) we find greater scepticism among the Chinese. A survey by J. McLenon provides further material for comparison[10]. McLenon surveyed about 800 students at three universities in the PRC, mainly focusing on out-of-the-body experiences and paranormal phenomena. Rather in contrast to what one might expect from our survey, he found a relatively high level of credence in such phenomena, 55% reporting out of the body experiences, 76% believing in the existence of a 'sixth sense' and 40% believing in the possibility of communicating with the dead. Although the questions were not exactly the same as ours, McLenon's results could suggest a higher level of scepticism among the students abroad.

A key question in many surveys has been on religious experience, as our question 15. Different surveys have asked "Have you ever felt somehow in the presence of God?", "Have you ever felt you were somehow in close contact with something holy?" and "Have you ever been aware of or influenced by a presence or power different from your everyday self?" The last wording was used in a major British survey[11]. Replies were: once or twice 18%, several times 10%, often 8%, negative (never) 64%. Results similar to this have been found in many surveys in Europe and the USA, with some form of positive answer generally lying between 30-50%.

This also corresponds to our data (positive ca. 36%) which is perhaps surprising given the low level of commitment to religions. It appears to suggest a high incidence of religious or unusual experiences as compared to formal religious commitment. Other information to emerge from Hay's work is that women generally report positive on this question in the ratio of 1.5:1 compared to men, confirming the popular intuition that women are less heathen than men (this was not confirmed in our survey); and that data strongly contradict the hypothesis that religious experience is more common among the poor and dispossessed. In fact the opposite is true: it is positively related to social class and education, to psychological health (on the Bradburn scale) and also to increased age. With regard to our survey group this might produce some contradictory tendencies. Students abroad are high in social class and education, which might tend to make them high scorers in religious experience. On the other hand they will have undergone more years of scientific and/or Marxist study, which might tend to work against religious belief.

Finally, Paffard in his indepth survey of British sixth formers and undergraduates found that ca. 75% of respondents (more females than males) practised a religion and ca. 75% attempted creative art[12]. He found those who

10. McLenon J. "A Study of Chinese Anomalous Experiences and Comparison with Western Representative National Samples", in *Journal for the Scientific Study of Religion*, Vol 27 No 3, 1988.
11. Hay D. and A. Morisy "Reports of Ecstatic, Paranormal or Religious Experience in Great Britain and the United States – A Comparison of Trends", in *Journal for the Scientific Study of Religion*, Vol 17 No 3, 1978.
12. Paffard, op. cit.

did attempt art were more likely to report religious experience, although he also raised the possibility that this was because of their greater confidence in expressing themselves. An interesting point for comparison with our survey was the written comments Paffard received concerning the nature of religious experience in response to a passage somewhat similar to ours in question 18. About 15% referred unambiguously to a personal God, conceived in specifically Christian, monotheistic terms, and another large group used language with overt religious connotations. Other common themes were a sense of mystery, importance and value attached to unusual experiences, and many references to poets and musicians including especially Beethoven, Bach and Wordsworth. By comparison, our respondents very rarely mentioned God; a more typical response was:

> "Very often nature scenery gives me calm, peace, courage and a sense of beauty. I enjoy this harmony . . . The wonderful feeling is generated by the resonance between nature and one's deep internal consciousness."

Paffard's collection of responses points to the abiding influence of Christian beliefs and the work of a handful of artists, especially Romantics and classical composers, on his group of young people. (This was the case at least in 1973 – one wonders how much has changed since then.) If we also consider the great contrast in religious commitment comparing our data with data from surveys of western populations, we must surely recognize highly significant differences at a deep level of consciousness between people nurtured in Chinese and western cultures. This question and its implications are clearly exceedingly complex. As a tentative first step towards a deeper analysis we can now consider the additional information received as comments on the questionnaire.

Analysis of Comments

As well as providing yes/no answers, respondents were requested to comment on their replies in several open-ended questions. Approximately 70 out of the 112 kindly did so, providing further interesting material. We collated these answers, having translated ten from Chinese (noted here by [C]), and attempted to unravel underlying themes. As noted already, ca. 20% clearly indicated an adherence to a 'scientistic' viewpoint. Many of these comments were variations on the theme that man has made God and that religions are illusions. To quote a few examples:

"It is our human beings who created God!"
"No way can be used to verify whether God/spirits exist or not."
"Seeing is believing."
"Life is only a natural phenomenon. It is the result of the long term combination and evolution of different chemical elements. There are not any kinds of gods or superforces which can invent life. Gods or any spirits are only invented

by human beings but do not really exist in the world or cosmos. Religious feelings can be explained by one branch of science, e.g. psychology."
"As a person studying natural sciences the only thing that can convince me to believe something is logical evidence. I am not interested in religion or atheism, they make no difference to me. Religions might be true to a certain extent because no-one can disprove them."

Similar views were expressed with regard to life after death:

"After death, physical body decays, spiritually nothing exists."
"All religions try to convince people of the existence of another life after death, this may fool people who are either stupid or innocent, but scientists should not surrender to this."
"I don't believe there is life after death. Human do like animals: when he die, he die forever."

Likewise with fortune-telling and prayer:

"Statistical analysis will show that the same type of people will have the similar fortune."
"If anybody gets any answers from God/spirits they are only hallucinations, reflecting his desires or anxieties."
"Prayers can always be explained by the psychological nature of the human being."

Among this positivist trend there were somewhat different assessments of religions' social functions. A few upheld the Leninist idea that religion is a tool for the exploiting classes:

"Mother Teresa's view, in my opinion, is very stupid. Her view was again expressed when she was interviewed by Time magazine no. 49 of this year. I think she is not a "pencil in the hand of God" but rather a pencil in the hand of anyone, especially tyrant, to fool the poor people to feel content about themselves."
"Ultimately all religions are harmful because they are irrational and superstitious. The world can only be saved by the reason of people, not by religions which have no sound logical foundation."

However, another type of response, even among the 'scientists' who had little personal interest in religions, was to accept that religions might have a beneficial social impact in some cases:

"I am not a religious person, in fact I believe in science. But if religions can make the world peaceful and make everybody happy, why not?"
"Although religions, in my view, are based on unscientific assumptions, their essences are love, peace and mercy (for most religions) which are indispensable

to our human society. But the result that religion has brought about is complicated: sometimes makes people merciful and friendly, sometimes makes people blind."

"I do not believe any religious interpretation of the world. But I think religion is useful in modern social life. The real value of religion relies on its moral force to maintain social order."

"It seems to me that people who believe in something (except hardline communists) behave better than hooligans."

"I see religion as offering moral norms for people's behaviour in society."

"I don't believe at all in religion's myths. But I'm interested in those parts that would give love, power, idealism, hope . . . I admire the possibility of a religion to give people faith and organization. [C]"

It is not surprising to find such attitudes among the Chinese elite. Even in traditional China there was a powerful tradition of atheism and scepticism, which included a strong hostility to Christianity. These attitudes were re-inforced by the contacts with western positivism in the May 4th movement, when the philosophers Russell and Dewey were warmly received by the Chinese intellectuals. From the 1920s 'science' became almost a creed in Chinese progressive circles, as it had been in Europe some decades earlier, with Darwin's theory of evolution being particularly popular.

Of course from the 1930s the paradigm has been subjected to serious criticism in western thought. It has been argued that positivism and the over-valuation of 'scientific method' is another ideology rather than a final truth, and this way of thinking was given the disparaging names 'scientism' and even 'scientolatry'. Important aspects of the postivist view were identified as:

1. a fundamental aversion to metaphysical thinking – only statements subject to empirical verification are considered valid;
2. science is considered to deal with empirical facts that are independent of the human subject;
3. judgements of value or morality are seen as meaningless: social comment should be neutral with respect to values;
4. the procedures of natural sciences are applicable to all spheres of life and culture;
5. there is deep emotional attachment to the alleged superiority of science over other modes of knowledge.

Several factors contributed to a critique of these tenets: the discoveries of theoretical physics, advances in the sociology and philosophy of science, greater reticence in using theories from one discipline as metaphors to discuss other areas of human life. Nevertheless positivist thinking is still influential, partly due to the immense prestige of technology in our society. It is easy to see why it has survived vigorously in China. It is fully compatible with orthodox Marxist-Leninism which is itself a fine example of nineteenth century scientism. Moreover it combines well with a hostility to organized religions, especially where it is complemented by a Leninist analysis of the class basis of religion. As has been suggested by Kwok in his analysis of scientism in China, the CCP wanted to achieve a world that would 'negate all past, obscurantist and unscientific worlds' and saw scientific thought as an important ally in this undertaking[13].

It was perhaps more surprising to find comments at the other end of the spectrum, namely appreciation of religious or spiritual ideals. It seemed that these did not form such a coherent set as the positivist comments, but most touched on the benefits that a religious outlook, in broad terms, might have for the individual or for society. Many emphasised the need for moral values and the contribution religions could make in this respect:

"When people are alive they should always help others and make all people happy and gay. The aim is in this world there should be nobody who is worried about their food and home at least. But there are too much troubles in the present world. I do not know if there is a God or Buddha in heaven. Anyway if people are religious there are more kind persons in this world. All people should love and help each other."

"Religion, especially Christianity, make people more kind and make their relationship more harmonious. It is certainly a good thing, although nobody can really prove there is God in heaven."

"Sometimes I feel a sudden spiritual uplift, especially by some spiritual love from somebody else. There is a co-existence of love and hatred in the world but I believe one can be better off to love rather than to hate or stay indifferent."

"Economic help is only one sort of help. Spiritual power is also a sort of help and sometimes may be more useful than economic help. There is a lack of love between ordinary people in China. Religion is interesting and useful to societies."

Hardly anyone wrote positively about fortune-telling, prayer or life after death, except for the rather condescending comment that: "Maybe fortune-teller can give some consolation to poor or unfortunate people". However, there were some lively replies concerning religion in education and its impact on young people, ranging from criticism of indoctrination to a plea for more freedom in China. One aspect mentioned by several people was that they were interested in religion but felt so deeply affected by many years of atheist education that they could never change:

"I find some religious people are crazy at convincing other people to follow their religion. I hate this. Let people decide for themselves...Teaching religion at school is wrong, very wrong indeed. Children have the right to decide what they should believe."

"Communist party kill all your belief except Marxism. In school we are taught all religions are evil. If anyone can dare to think, will be killed."

13. D. Kwok, *Scientism in China 1900-1950*, New Haven: Yale University Press, 1965, p.100. For a survey of scientism and positivism in western social sciences, particularly religious studies, see B. Morris, *Anthropological Studies of Religion*, Cambridge University Press, 1987, pp. 51-54.

"Since I was brought up in such a way I think it is impossible to believe in a religion. But I wish I did. I understand people with religion and I hope that Chinese children when they are in school can be taught different ideology rather than communism alone and given the right to choose a religion as they like."

Perhaps the most interesting set of comments were those in response to the passages and the open question. It is hard to define the overall 'feel' of the replies which were, naturally, different for each individual. Two themes were repeated which are perhaps worth noting: an appreciation of balance, harmony, the natural world; and the suggestion that spiritual feelings are essentially a human phenomenon rather than a specifically religious one:

"It seems to me that I have had such experiences not just once or twice but nearly in every stage of my life, and some of them have been significant factors in my life. But I am not quite sure whether they were religious or rather mental, aesthetic experiences."

"World needs love, people need goodness, but that is normal human being not religion."

"People should love each other, but this is something different from the love of Christ."

"This kind of feeling does not necessarily have anything to do with religion. Spiritual strength is something that everyone needs apart from the physical and material side of the world. . . . The good part of any religion is actually the virtues common to all human beings. The good virtues do not exist just within the realm of religion. On the contrary it seems that it is religion which has incorporated these virtues."

"I think love and compassion are the symbols of being, the basic principles of a person's life."

"Life is a search for balance. There is time for you to cry and time for you to be happy. You need to control your own life and that strength essentially comes from yourself. Of course external factors are influential but nor decisive. Life is too short, you have to be optimistic about the future."

"On a fine evening, look at the starry sky. The stars smile, soft moonlight floods the earth, a stream babbles under the shadows of leaves – all of them play on the quiet earth a melody in praise of eternity. From this we can realise the smallness of life and the vastness of the universe. I went to the countryside after high school and laboured from morning to night like a robot. Every time I became sick from the meaningless, compulsive routine I wandered alone in the dark night along the river, moonshine on my shoulders, among the bushes. From the grass I looked at the starry sky and the meaning of life dawned upon me. Revelation gave me hope and courage to wait for a beautiful future. The universe is beautiful, serene and harmonious. Human life should also be like this." [C]

"The enlightening power of nature's transcendent light and the beautiful feelings it can evoke from man's consciousness are beyond rational recognition. These things are hard to trace back to their origins. But religious feelings are a part of human feelings. Any crackdown on it can only lead to distortion." [C]

"Nature is beautiful. It can cure any spiritual wounds. Nature and love are the most important things in life."

Such passages, along with many others which cannot be quoted here, are representative of the 'pro-religionists' in our group. We need far more data about the quality of contemporary Chinese spirituality, but here will venture some speculative remarks. Readers will not need reminding that from the origins of Chinese literature a major theme has been the resonance between human consciousness and the natural world, harmony between the human being (generally male and member of the élite) and nature. Perhaps in the comments quoted above we see the abiding influence of classical poetry, much as Paffard found Christian and Romantic sentiments deeply influential among young westerners. Perhaps also one could discern the impact of western culture: the emphasis on love, for example, may be a 'western import'; or does it come from an alternative Chinese tradition, a legacy of Wang Yangming or other thinkers? Remembering our earlier findings, it seems reasonable to state that there is widespread recognition of spiritual experience among our Chinese group, and that is interpreted and expressed in ways that differ from what one would expect to find in a western culture. It is interesting to observe the possible intrusion of western concepts on the Chinese consciousness as a counterpart to the fascination with eastern spirituality that has affected Europe and America since the 1960s.
Finally, many remarks were hard to classify, sometimes enigmatic, sometimes humourous. It is easy to speak of the 20% 'positivists' and 20% 'pro-religionists' but these are only approximate terms. All respondents are individuals, probably reflective, serious and sensitive, and of course the 60% 'non-aligned' may well be the most thoughtful of them all: one impression gained from the survey was that most of these people had not stopped inquiry, they were not satisfied with ready-made answers. A few random comments are included here:

"In China people could not often be happy, they are generally worried about family difficulties, especially when the political movement was coming. Love from wife and childrn was the most important factor to overcome these difficulties. I could not depend on love from other Chinese people, even a close friend, because he would not hesitate to lose my benefits so that he could be trusted by the governor, the political leaders."
"I do not believe any religions now. I may believe Buddhism or Christianity when I am older."
"I suspect if the people concerned in these two paragraphs [Question 18] had ever suffered real miserable life."
"We should do our best to help and love people. Since all of us come to this world together everyone has right to enjoy it. I should re-establish the idea of religion, i.e. what is religion, whether it is just about God, is this all its content? I need to have a new idea. I think some Chinese students also need this."
[On prayer] "I have tried but nobody answered."
"God loves all people who believe in him. But I think he has forgotten the Chinese."

One respondent had a request which we shall use as a conclusion to this section, in the hope that some reader may be able to oblige:

"There is no-one so far give me a clear and convincing answer about what God is and where God is from. If you can offer some help on this subject I would be very grateful."

Conclusion

In the first place, our survey suggests that Chinese students abroad can be profitably approached through a postal survey. They could be a valuable source of information concerning attitudes in this stratum of Chinese society or other issues.
Second, the following are the main hypotheses suggested by the limited data of our survey:
1. ca. 20% of young, highly educated Chinese are inclined to a scientistic worldview;
2. ca. 20% are inclined to a more idealist, perhaps religious, aesthetic or spiritual standpoint;
3. the other 60% show some degree of interest in religious matters and are not generally hostile to religion;
4. very few are strongly committed to a particular religion;
5. demographic variables make little difference to this pattern, except that
6. children of religious parents are more likely to be sympathetic towards religions;
7. there is little belief in life after death, petitionary prayer or fortune-telling;
8. there is considerable interest in a range of existential questions, particularly among students of social sciences and humanities and students who have attempted artistic work.
Third, we can identify some areas where further research would seem to be promising. For example, what is the relation between parents' belief and their childrens'? Does our overall assessment of 'religious orientation' stand up to further testing? Would it be possible to examine in greater detail the nature of the scientistic and idealist strands of belief that we have discussed? Is it true that demographic differences are relatively unimportant in determining Chinese student attitudes? The sociology of religion in China certainly demands further exploration.

APPENDIX – Synopsis of survey questions

Part One Demographic information
1. Age 2. Sex 3. Home town/province 4. Main subject of studies
5. Date of arrival in Britain 6. Apart from school assignments have you ever attempted artistic work? 7. Parents' religious beliefs (if any).
Part Two General attitudes

8. Which of the following best describes your feelings about religious belief: a) deep commitment/ b) interest and curiosity / c) not religious/ d) religion is superstitious and harmful/ e) none of these
9. Your attitude (true/ sympathetic interest/ neutral/ opposed) to the following religions: Christianity, Buddhism, Islam, Taoism/popular religions.
10. How much do you think about the following (often/sometimes/never): How did the world come into being? What is the purpose of life? How can I find real happiness? Why is there suffering in the world? What happens after death?
11. Are these questions important?
12. View of life after death: a) some belief/ b) belief, involves reward or punishment/ c) reincarnation/ d) unsure/ e) don't believe/ f) other
13. Could prayer to God/spirits ever be answered? (Definitely yes/possibly/ very doubtful/no).
14. Belief in fortune telling (definitely yes/possibly/very doubtful/no).
Part 3 Personal experience
15. Have you ever felt you were in close contact with something holy or beyond normal human consciousness? (often/sometimes/never)
16. Did any particular person, event or experience influence your beliefs?
17. What were you taught about religions at school and at home?
18. Two passages concerning spiritual feelings were provided, one concerning a mystical experience in relation to nature and the other reporting some words by Mother Teresa.
Do these passages remind you of anything you ever felt? Please comment.
19. Please explain any further feelings you have about religion or atheism.

Worth giving some attention to in review.

8. CHRISTIAN HUMANISM AND DEMOCRACY IN CHINA: A VIEW FROM HONG KONG

Carver Yu

Introduction

For more than seventy years since the May Fourth Movement, science and democracy have been the guiding stars for Chinese intellectuals in their quest for national and cultural reconstruction. Yet unfortunately in the process of that quest, science has taken on a form of scientism that tramples on traditional Chinese humanistic values, and democracy has become no more than a name to facilitate totalitarian control of the people. The scientistic-mechanistic world-view developed in the name of science and the collectivist understanding of human society have worked together to reduce the human person to a functional element in either a socio-political or a historical process. Not only is the human person no longer the subject of history, he/she is no longer the subject of his/her own self, which has become a cog of the party or the state machine. The personal "I" has become a mere grammatical "I"[1].

The quest for science and democracy needs to start afresh, and in both instances the human person has to stand out as a distinct reality which cannot be reduced to anything other than itself. It is our conviction that both the Chinese and the Christian humanistic traditions have much to contribute to this. In our discussion here, we shall concentrate on the quest for democracy.

The Relevance of the Chinese Tradition

Plato, when discussing the ideal political system in The Laws, first articulates the fundamental principle that sovereign authority should not be vested in a person or a class but in impersonal law[2]. He then takes up the apparently unrelated subject of reverence[3]. This is, however, no accident, for to Plato, the law is grounded in reverence of those for whom the law is legislated, and the discussion on reverence may therefore be regarded as the preamble to the law. Also, the discussion which begins with reverence to parents, then to fellow-men, ends in reverence to one's own soul. In other words, the corner-stone of good government is reverence for the human person.

This is the heart of the Chinese humanistic tradition in which all moral cultiva-

1. Arthur Koestler, *Darkness at Noon*, Harmondsworth: Penguin, 1978.
2. Plato, *The Laws*, 713e.
3. Ibid., 721a-734d.

tion aims precisely at reverence of the human person. Very often, the essence of Chinese culture is thought to be a set of moral ideals that govern human relations, but this interpretation of the Chinese tradition fails to grasp the metaphysical and religious depth of the Chinese spirit. Indeed, the Chinese have put great emphasis on the practice of moral ideals, but the emphasis on practice is grounded in the fundamental perception of Being. It is in moral practice that Being may unfold itself. When one acts morally, one is actualizing the way of Being. Being is not there to be known cognitively, but is unfolded in one's inner self and in the very depth of one's humanity. That is, Being is grasped in its very actualization or concretization in authentic human existence[4]. Here, Being and the knowledge of Being become unified. In the Chinese tradition, knowledge of this kind is called *xin xing zhi xue* (the study of heart and nature), and only knowledge of this kind is regarded as true knowledge. One knows Being in the authentic acting out of what is natural to one's heart and nature *xin xing*. In other words, the essence of Chinese culture lies in the conviction that humanity is the locus for the actualization of Being. It is a conviction that when one goes into the depth of 'humanity', one 'touches' Being itself. That is to say, the essential insight of Chinese culture is the fundamental affirmation of the significance of humanity in the unfolding drama of Being. Any development of science or struggle for democracy has to keep in view this affirmation of humanity in order to be true to the very nature of science and democracy[5].

According to contemporary Chinese philosophers like Tang Junyi and Mou Zongsan, the problem with western culture arises from the Greek and Christian humanistic spirit having given way to realism and naturalism. Through the naturalistic spirit, westerners reduce human beings to things[6]. Therefore the spirit that has made science possible is submerged in a world of things. The root of the problem, according to Tang, lies in the western attempt to see the world abstracted from its fundamental relation with the human[7]. Westerners attempt to see a 'pure world', 'a world without the person who is perceiving it'[8]. In so doing they have to suppress the human spirit, and they forget that the world which is to be circumscribed is precisely a world with the human spirit[9]. The result is clear: they exchange the humanized world for an alien world of natural objects. In contrast to the western philosophic tradition in which one is constantly compelled to prove the existence of the external world or the existence of the subject himself, the Chinese approach to reality begins with *jing* (reverence)[10]. *Jing* is the intuitive confidence of the existence, as well as the infinite

4. Carsun Chang, *Development of Neo-Confucian Thought*, New York: Bookman Associates, 1962, Vol 2, pp. 455-84.
5. Tang Junyi (T'ang Chun-i), *Zhonghua ren wen yu dangqian shijie*, (Chinese Culture and the Contemporary World), Taipei 1975, pp. 895-910.
6. Tang Junyi (T'ang Chun-i), *Ren wen jingshen zhi chongjian* (The Reconstruction of the Spirit of Humanity), Hong Kong, 1974, pp. 157 ff.
7. Ibid., p. 166.
8. Ibid., p. 41
9. Ibid., p. 42.
10. Cf. Tang Junyi (T'ang Chun-i) *Zhongguo wenhua zhi jingshen jiazhi* (The Spiritual Values of Chinese Culture), Taipei, 1951, pp. 136ff.

value, of humanity and the cosmos. From this intuitive confidence springs a deep sense of reverence.

Jing was originally a religious concept, referring to the feeling of 'mysterium tremendum', but it was later transformed into a political concept[11], the virtue of a ruler. A ruler had to revere *tian* (heaven), but heaven was not a remote, abstract concept; rather, it was immanent in the people. Therefore reverence for Heaven was identical with reverence for the people. *Jing* was then further extended into the wider context of human relations and of the human relation to the cosmos. With their intuitive reverence for the human as well as for the cosmos, Chinese philosophers did not need to be preoccupied with proving the existence of both the world and the human; rather they were concerned with how they should relate to them in reverence. Here, the idea of *ren* (humanity) comes into the picture[12]. From the intuitive awareness of the infinite value of all that is, one has to relate to everything according to the way of *ren*. When one attains ren, one reaches a state of communion with all things. Through such communion, not only is the person enriched, but the thing he/she is in communion with is also enriched[13]. With the cultivation of *ren*, the problem of suppression and exploitation of others is resolved, and this lays the spiritual foundation for a good government. The basis of good government starts therefore with the cultivation of the sense of reverence for, and the sense of communion with, others. Given the existence of these philosophical insights, one may ask why something that comes close to the democratic spirit has never emerged in China, and what spiritual elements fundamental to democracy are lacking in the Chinese tradition. These questions point us to the relevance of the Christian humanistic tradition to the Chinese quest for democracy.

The Relevance of the Christian Tradition

Both Plato and Aristotle considered three forms of government, monarchy, aristocracy, and polity as potentially good forms of government. Their deviant forms, tyranny, oligarchy and democracy, are considered as bad forms of government. Monarchy is the rule of one man in accordance with the law; tyranny is the rule of one man in accordance with his own will. Aristocracy is the rule of a few in accordance with the law, while oligarchy is the rule of a few in accordance with their own will. Polity is the rule of the majority in accordance with the law, while democracy is the rule of the masses in accordance with their own will. It is quite clear that what distinguishes good forms of government

11. Cf. Mou Zongsan (Mou Tseng-san), *Zhongguo zhexue zhi tezhi*, (The Characteristics of Chinese Philosophy), Taipei, 1975, pp. 15ff.
12. *Ren* is one of the most fundamental concepts in Confucianism. It has been interpreted variously by different scholars to mean compassion for another human person, reciprocity and mutuality between persons,or benevolence or love, or humaneness. But none is adequate to express the full meaning. Perhaps, more accurately, it may be taken to mean the stage of full humanity or authentic human existence realized in and through human relations.
13. Mou, op. cit., p. 30.

from their distorted forms is rule by law as opposed to rule by arbitrary will. Law here cannot be mere positive legislation made only by consent or contract, but it points to something greater and deeper, to a law that is intrinsic to both nature and human nature and that can be discovered by reason. It points to an objective absolute truth that cannot be reduced by the subjective will. The opening words of the Declaration of Independence that "all men are created equal" points to an axiom that is not reached through common consent. It is a truth that reveals something more profound, and in it one can see the distinction that Plato made between polity and democracy. What we call democracy today Plato would regard as polity, but our democracy is in danger of being reduced to the rule of the majority in accordance with their will, regardless of whether their will takes into consideration the law of nature or of human nature. Endless economic growth ensuring prosperity for all may be the wish of the majority, but it may threaten to destroy nature and with it humanity altogether.

The Christian contribution goes beyond even this through the idea of the rule of human life and society by the divine Law. The Christian faith in God as the indissoluble and irreducible subject as well as the ground of rationality and order leads to the cultivation of an awareness of an irreducible, objective and absolute truth which transcends human subjectivity. With this awareness, one tends to look beyond oneself for an objective reference, and this awareness is essential to the rule by Law. The western quest for objective ultimate truth is of course closely linked to the quest in the Greek tradition for the most fundamental and universal principle, but the Christian belief in divine rationality - and therefore the rationality of the cosmos as well as the human - has also made a significant impact. The concept of revelation as a manifestation of God's subjectivity lays the ground for confidence in both the objectivity and the knowability of the ultimate.

The Christian concept of covenant is also significant. Even though human beings are confronted with God, with whom they are infinitely incomparable, yet God chooses to enter into a form of relation with them in which they are given the right to regard themselves as standing on an equal footing with God, as covenantal partners. The possibility for participation is open to humanity. Here, the absolutely objective, the law, is not thrust onto us, but internalized in us through our own identification with it. Through such participation the reality of human subjectivity can be actualized.

In Biblical history, it is the people who are the subject of history, and the concept of the people stands out as the dominant idea in the political experience of the Biblical world. This was perhaps somewhat revolutionary in the ancient world, where the people were usually regarded as possessions of kings. Since the people had a covenant with God, there was at least the theoretical possibility that Israel could be governed without kings. It was the people who decided the form of government at a critical moment in history (I Samuel 8); without the idea of the people being the subject, democracy could not have been developed. The ideal form of government in the Bible is theocracy. Theocracy may be regarded as absolutely totalitarian, for God has absolute power that no one can challenge. However the Biblical form of theocracy lays the spiritual foundation for democracy. First, God does not rule by arbitrary will, but in accordance with the law covenanted between God and the people. Even God is bound by the covenant. The freedom of the absolute God is manifested in acknowledged self-limitation. Freedom and self-limitation are thus paradoxically bound together for the true understanding of the liberty that is so vital to democracy. Perhaps, more important than this, the Hebrew form of theocracy denies any person any claim of superiority over his fellows. Only God stands above people to rule over them, and nobody is to rule over others. God's absoluteness relativizes all people, putting them on an equal footing.

At the same time, in the New Testament, all become unified and therefore totally equal in Christ, thus taking human equality even further. At the same time, the idea that Israel is to be a kingdom of priests leads on to the concept that each individual stands before the Absolute, being accountable to God as a responsive and responsible person. No one is to answer for that person standing before God as an individual. To be a priest is to represent God with one's life, a life to be taken with utmost seriousness, a life that is infinitely valuable in the eyes of God.

The idea that people are free agents given the possibility and reality of choice is another significant element in the Christian tradition which is relevant to the development of the democratic spirit. God did not create completely pre-determined human existence. The fact that we can revolt against God points to the reality of our freedom, and the freedom to sin is a positive indication of God's grace. According to I Samuel 8, humans were in fact even given the freedom to choose a form of government against which God issued a warning. In the event the first occasion for self-determination in choice of government came to pass with God's blessing. The people not only have the right to choose but the right to choose what is wrong in the eyes of God. The right to do wrong is thus given to human beings, and the Biblical theocratic society is an open society, where even the most fundamental rules can be changed through participation.

However, the awareness of the fact that power corrupts and absolute power corrupts absolutely is also revealed in I Samuel 8, where the negative consequences of domination over others are vividly described. In other places, human sin is also clearly revealed, pointing to the intrinsic danger in all human forms of government. Continual alertness and openness to self-criticism become highly significant, and God therefore builds into the political system of Israel the institution of self-criticism. The prophetic minority becomes the test of this alertness and openness. Prophets in Israel have a significant role to play as critics of the status quo. They are the minority; they are not only allowed to exist, but their existence becomes a mandate and is religiously guaranteed; and their integrity becomes the test of the soundness of society. They are the force for the renewal of society, and this tradition is a key factor in the development of the democratic spirit.

Finally, the idea of the leader being the servant is also highly significant for the development of the democratic spirit. Moses was keenly aware of the fact that it was the people and not he who was the subject of history. He was also aware of the fact that as leader the fulfilment of his task was to bring Israel to a state where leaders like him were obsolete. Rulers had to demonstrate their style and attitudes before the people, and Joshua, for instance, chose to present himself in exemplary fashion as a leader who would not impose himself upon his subjects. Servanthood was repeatedly stressed. Servant-like Moses was willing to die for the people. In Jesus Christ, the reality of servanthood was fully revealed and became the guiding principle for leadership.

The Christian Tradition In The Reconstruction Of The Chinese Humanistic Tradition

In light of the above discussion, a number of issues may be considered further. The Chinese humanistic spirit also embraces the idea of the ultimate, which is symbolized as Tao. Yet Tao cannot be said, cannot be named. When one is confronted with Tao, one is faced with something before which human concepts and human language fail completely. However, there is no need to search for Tao. The manifestation of Tao is in the human, and the human is the locus for the manifestation of Tao. According to Confucius: "It is not Tao which makes man great, but it is man which makes Tao great", because Tao finds its clearest manifestation in the human. Here the transcendent is immanent. Although there is an awareness that Tao which is immanent in the individual is also transcendent, the objective reality of Tao has never been clearly perceived except by the subject in his/her concrete situation. It is even a principle not to attempt to circumscribe Tao. This awareness of the limitation of human concepts and language is deeply appreciated; but in some respects it may hinder the Chinese mind from perceiving the objective absolute. There is in fact a tendency in the Chinese tradition to 'subjectivize' the truth.

Since the human being in many respects is the embodiment of Tao, there is less incentive to look beyond oneself than if one stands before the judgment of the absolute Other. This may hinder the development of an openness to something other than oneself. In the Chinese tradition, moments of manifestation of Tao in concrete situations are very significant, but such spiritual insights again may dampen the desire to formulate general eternal universal principles[14]. The idea of the law being the ultimate objective reference has yet to be developed as a possible means to lay the foundation of democracy. In this respect, the Christian faith in God as the indissoluble subject and the ultimate ground of rational order both in the cosmos and in the human world may have a message for the Chinese tradition. To some degree, human beings have divine absoluteness, yet they are forever confronted with a reality which is much more profound, a reality which is approachable and knowable through revelation.

14. Sheng Gao, a mathematician in ancient China, had long before Pythagoras discovered the relationship among the three sides of the right angled triangle. However, what he discovered was a particular case, that is, when one side is of three units of measure, and the other is of four units, then the third side must be of five units. Sheng Gao never really managed to draw the general principle from this particular case. It was Pythagoras who grasped it as a general principle.

Human life is indeed highly valued in the Chinese tradition, but the concept of the human being as an individual has yet to develop fully. In China, humans have always existed in relation to each other, and the context of relations defines the reality of their existence, which very often is a configuration of social roles. The human beings of the Bible do exist in relation to each other, but they are also covenantal partners who enter into the covenant through the exercise of their will. The covenant becomes real only when they choose to enter into it. Here, the reality of subjectivity becomes all the more distinct in the act of covenanting.

The idea of the freedom of the will does not seem to be very distinct in the Chinese tradition in contrast with Western culture. The problem of freedom and determinism, and the tragic sense of life in the realization of the human being as a free agent, do not seem to have been important themes either in Chinese philosophy or literature. In the West, the problem of Liberum Arbitrium is still one of vital debate after many centuries; the tragic sense of human struggle against bondage is also strong. All this contributes to the Western consciousness of the human being as an individual responsible for personal choices. Freedom of choice is a gift from God to be covetously guarded.

The idea of the corruption of humanity has never been taken very seriously in the Chinese tradition. Thus the need to take measures to safe-guard ourselves from such corruption has not been fully appreciated. The concept of the balance of power and the legitimacy of opposition also need to be developed as political ideas in China. The Christian tradition has fostered political realism out of its awareness of the sinful nature of humanity. All human institutions have to stand before judgment and criticism. The prophetic tradition symbolizes opposition to power. In the Chinese quest for democracy, some fundamental elements in the Christian tradition may emerge as highly significant in complementing China's own spiritual and social values.

– don't include in review, unless re-read 1st.

9. WHAT HAS CHANGED? A VIGNETTE OF SHANTOU

George A. Hood

As the boat from Hong Kong entered the wide expanse of Shantou harbour we passed the island of Masu, known to the foreign community as 'Double Island' because of its twin peaks, and home of the foreign opium merchants and smugglers before Shantou, the outlet for the Chaozhou Fu city, became a Treaty Port in 1860. More distantly, twenty miles away, we could make out the higher peaks of Nanao Island. Once a Chinese Naval Station, the island in the 1830s had also accommodated a major distribution centre for the opium provided by the fast moving lorchas of Jardine and Matheson. Houses had been built and a race course laid out for the traders' benefit before the Treaty of Nanjing in 1842 more clearly defined the rights to be conceded, which at that stage did not include this favourite location. That had not prevented the trade continuing but by 1860 Shantou and Masu had overtaken Nanao as the main centre for the now legalized import.

From Nanao, Rudolph Lechler of the Basel Mission, beguiled by Gutzlaff's[1] enthusiastic accounts of successful evangelism along the China coast, had begun work on the mainland in 1848. Five years later, disillusioned both with Gutzlaff and the latter's Chinese Union, and facing increased hostility from the local officials, he had abandoned his work. But some of his converts reappeared after the English Presbyterian and American Baptist missionaries renewed the missionary attempt in Shantou and on Masu from 1858 onwards.

It was on Masu that the arrival of the first British consul, G.W. Caine, in 1860, had been heralded with a salute of seven guns followed by another of twenty when the Union Jack was hoisted over the temporary consulate. Within two weeks the consul was involved in a more deadly display of fire power in the use of his gunboats against pirates who had captured a French Catholic priest and held him to ransom. Other incidents had followed and it had been five years before the consul had achieved his objective, an official visit to the Fu city, only thirty miles inland, The local prefect was under pressure from Beijing to carry out the terms of the Treaty of Tianjin which had conceded a further group of Treaty Ports, including Shantou. But in the face of opposition from the local

1. Charles Gutzlaff, the maverick missionary, whose passion to evangelize China led him to employment by Jardine and Matheson on their opium smuggling boats, and later to service as Chinese Secretary in Hong Kong, had made a deep impression in European evangelical circles, first by his *Journal of Three Voyages along the Coast of China in 1831, 1832 and 1833*, and later in the 1840s by the successes in evangelism he claimed both for himself and the Chinese Union he had organized. In response to his appeal for support, Hamberg and Lechler were sent out to Hong Kong by the Basel Mission in 1847.

gentry, experts in arousing popular anti-foreign feeling, he had had to tread a delicate path lest he also incurred too much hostility from those who had a reputation for easily becoming ungovernable.

On that boat in 1983 there were four British among the several hundred Chinese passengers. It was an emotional experience. Many of our Chaozhou fellow passengers were making their first return journey from Thailand and other areas of South East Asia. We all lined the sides of the boat, vainly trying to identify buildings along a water front which had changed beyond recognition. The British were two couples, a small family group, my wife and her brother, his wife and myself. Brother and sister had been born in Shantou, grandchildren of William and Margaret Duffus, two of the earliest Presbyterian missionaries in that area, who had served there from 1869 to 1892, and children of parents who had followed the same calling from 1908 to 1935. My wife and I had served there as missionaries for a much shorter time, from 1945 to 1950, but equally full of incident, and when we left we had still hoped there would be a place for us in 'New China'. The Korean War and what followed had ended that hope. Now as 'old foreign friends' we had been invited to return and visit what was, at least in the case of my wife and her brother, something akin to their 'native village'.

When the boat came alongside the quay we were courteously shepherded down the gangway and were the first to pass through the customs formalities. It was a quiet and orderly experience in sharp contrast to those struggles of bygone days when the sampans circulated the boat competing for the lucrative business of unloading the foreigners' baggage; memories of a trunk which had fallen between the big boat and the surrounding sampans came to mind. The officers examining passports were quite satisfied with a Chinese name hurriedly bestowed on my wife's sister in law, the only one who had not previously lived in China. Then we were through and out into the bright morning sunshine, carrying our bags into a long lane with a sea of faces behind a low barrier at the end of it. Everyone there was waiting for friends and relations. As we drew nearer there were hands waving and smiles of recognition. Thirty-three years had passed since we left. For the first thirty of them there had been no communication from either end, and now it was as if nothing had changed in the warmth of feeling with which we were greeted.

Nothing had changed; everything had changed. During our time in Shantou and visiting the surrounding area with which we were familiar from former years, and then travelling to Zhangzhou, Xiamen, Hangzhou and Guangzhou, the basic question, appearing in a variety of forms, was still: what had changed, what remained the same? When I returned alone, six weeks later, after a time in Hong Kong to reflect on that first euphoric visit, it was the same question which was in my mind. I looked and listened while my Chinese friends shared with me some if not all of their experience over the past thirty years, and their high hopes for the future. Three years later, 1986, at the end of a much longer visit to other areas of China and the Church there, taking us from Beijing to Kunming, Suzhou to Yenan, and ending in Shantou, it was the same question which persisted, at various levels: what had changed, what remained the same?

To the outward eye it was nearly all change both between 1950 and 1983 and between 1983 and 1986. The waterfront, unrecognizable in 1983, had undergone still further development in 1986. The old town of Shantou was extended both by land reclaimed from the harbour, with high buildings now rising on it, and equally dramatically by the new Special Economic Zone to the east. Shantou, now a city of nearly half a million, a product of the nineteenth century which owed so much in its early growth to the opium trade, had finally usurped in importance the old city of Chaozhou. Whereas forty years before almost all transport was by water, now roads radiated in every direction, and as you travelled along them in a minibus you could see the prosperity in the villages, represented by the number of new houses in process of building, some only awaiting the profits from the next harvest for their completion. There was the same impression of change in the formerly impoverished mountain villages fifty miles inland, where brightly clothed and well shod school children were now to be seen instead of the buffalo-minding ill-clothed urchins of former years. In place of a drying ground of beaten earth for the grain there was smooth cement, and along with it life-transforming running water and electricity. And by 1986 the Shantou University projected in 1983 was already built and functioning through the munificence of Hong Kong's wealthiest business man, a son of Chaozhou.

What about the Christian community in 1983 whom we had come to visit as old friends? In some ways, again to the outward eye and ear, the lack of change was as surprising as those changes already described. Very little had altered in the style and content of worship. Robed choirs still sang the same introits and anthems, and the order of service with its emphasis on biblical expository preaching was the same as before. Perhaps there was a greater degree of concentrated reverence, a feature which seemed to impress those, many of them young, whose previous experience of crowded gatherings was limited to political meetings.

To see friends who have come from a distance has always ranked high in Chinese cultural tradition. In this case, as those who had come, we were seeing again many of whom nothing had been heard, and some of these had been presumed dead. In fact it was clear that the passing of the years had taken a greater toll of fellow missionaries than of our Chinese colleagues. We were shamed when we realized that some of the former whom we had forgotten were still remembered in China, a reminder that to remember is a well developed Chinese characteristic.

There were some missing faces, and although the Cultural Revolution was blamed for most of what was tragic, both personally and nationally, it was clear that there was also another history which was not yet ready to be fully described. Personal experience of public humiliation and persistent interrogation, of the destruction of church property, bibles, hymnbooks, furnishings, records, and of the struggle for physical survival, was recounted with a mixture of humour and tolerance, but untinged by romanticism. Among the former students in the theological school where I had taught, many had become teachers in government service, some were now reaching retirement and able to contemplate giving full time service to the Church. A small number had served the Church throughout the whole period. Several others had become Party members, but not all of these had lost contact with their former fellow students. How strong the bond remains of those who study together!

That first visit was emotional and euphoric, visiting familiar places and meeting people, some of whom could recall our forebears as well as ourselves, seeing the material progress and hearing the high hopes being entertained. It was still the early stages of the Church's rehabilitation, and more often than not the Christians whom we met were negotiating for the return of their buildings. Clearly our travel to see so many churches in the rural hinterland was done with the approval of the Religious Affairs Bureau, with whom the church leaders in Shantou had established a high degree of mutual trust in the past thirty years, one benefit from the immobility affecting both government and church appointments. In one country town I was asked to speak at a large house meeting where the minister was known to me and had been there since before Liberation. But in most places our words were limited to responding, all too inadequately, to the kind and generous hospitality we received and in sharing reminiscences of people and experiences long ago.

When I returned on my own six weeks later I was more aware of the remaining gaps in my knowledge of what had happened in the previous thirty three years, and hoped that by patient listening, without asking too many leading questions, those gaps would be filled. This hope was partly realized but I remained convinced that the tempo of communication and explanation should be set by the hosts and not the guest.

One friend of former days who had spent almost all his life teaching English brought a group of his brightest students to the hotel where I was staying for an experience of genuine English conversation. Before agreeing to this I had made sure that my friends among the Christian leaders understood that I had no intention of surreptitious evangelism. Not long before, 'Brother Andrew' of Bible smuggling fame had supposedly landed nearly half a million copies of the Bible on the shore near Shantou. Although the incoming tide had been as effective as the police and customs officials in dealing with these modern day smuggled goods, an unhappy echo of Shantou's earlier reputation, this action had been a serious embarrassment to the Christian leaders in their relations with government officials. I was determined not to betray their confidence in me, nor to undermine the Three Self Principle, nor to raise suspicion about my teacher friend. Three years later, in 1986, the same friend was happy to introduce me to his headmaster and I gave an English lesson in the classroom.

During that earlier visit one of the most moving conversations I had was with another friend who had served in our house as a young man, and concerned the remarkable growth of a village congregation of which he was a member. Before this visit I had heard from him that within the previous two years there had been one hundred and forty adult baptisms, the kind of growth quite unheard of in former days. I was anxious to hear from his own lips how this had come about. At first he would only ascribe it to the work of the Holy Spirit. When I pressed him further and asked if there was any significant time or happening from which it began, he hesitatingly referred to the sad loss he and his family had experienced through the death of his son. That seemed to be the time at which many others in the village had begun to seek out the small group of Christians. I hesitated to ask more and was content to make my own suppositions. Was it the way in which the Christian family had faced a human tragedy which was universally understood, the manner in which they had cared for him and for each other, the acceptance in faith of what had happened? Most significantly it had not been a miraculous cure but the reverse which had been a turning point.

When my wife and I returned to the Shantou area in 1986 it was for ten days at the end of a long period of travel in other parts of China. During those ten days, in which we visited fifteen congregations, the most illuminating experience was the weekend spent in the company of the Religious Affairs Bureau officials in a neighbouring county which we had also visited three years before. We travelled there in the Christian Council's minibus and stayed in the same hotel as the cadres. We visited the senior cadre's room to pay our respects, and subsequently had most meals together, along with some of the local church elders. On the Sunday morning we visited together the Catholic Church and the Buddhist Temple before the Protestant Church service. It was clear that all the religious bodies shared some practical problems and took the opportunity to air them both for the RAB cadres and our own benefit. We also passed a shrine dedicated to 'popular religion', and in answer to my enquiry the official explained that so long as its activities were not exploitative of human weaknesses and credulity, using religion for personal material profit, they were not interfered with. Before the church service proper began, the minister, one of my former students, invited me to say a few words to the congregation of five hundred, and I gave them greetings from Christians in Britain and in particular from 'Friends of the Church in China'[2] of which at that time I was chairman. The RAB cadres who attended the service were most interested to learn of this body which was demonstrably not a missionary society but was so interested in Christians in China. A meeting of Church lay workers, young and old, was held in the evening at which the RAB stressed the Three Self Principle, and particularly urged upon those present their financial responsibilities for support of the ministry, and the need of more young people to seek training.

In meetings and conversations such as these the different character of the Christian community became clearer, what had really changed more evident. ~i.e. ? The role of the Church in China's modernization offered further illustration. A small town congregation was employing nearly 100 young people in a clothing factory on the church premises, and most of these were also members of the church choirs. Christians in Shantou were running a highly regarded kindergarten. On church premises there was a free clinic staffed by retired Christian medical personnel, and also, more surprisingly, a branch of one national bank which Christians had been asked to staff. The former Church Middle School had been allowed to resume its original name and was seeking, I was told, to recover the high reputation it had enjoyed in earlier years. Similar concern was ex-

2. The 'Friends of the Church in China' is an ecumenical fellowship of Christians, inaugurated in 1984, to deepen understanding between Christians in the British Isles and China, on the basis of mutual trust and respect.

pressed relating to the former 'Christian Hospitals' which had been in government hands for over thirty years. Alongside all this revaluing of an earlier Christian social service there was the undeniable growth in the number of those seeking church membership. Before Liberation this had been an area of 100 years of intensive Protestant missionary effort, mainly English Presbyterian and American Baptist, covering most of the towns and larger villages, so that proportionately it was one of the most Christian areas of China, but even so progress had been slow, and those added were not in the numbers now seeking baptism. This was change; what had caused it?

If it was clear that neither the content nor form of worship had changed, if the same preaching and teaching was being heard, if the Christian virtues which had always been consistent with much of the Confucian tradition were still being pursued, if the Chinese Christian's claim to patriotism was no longer suspect, then it must be that all this was happening in a new context and a changed relationship of Christians to the community in which they lived. In the rural areas small groups of Christians, often just a few families in a large village belonging to the church, had once experienced alienation from the life of the community. Their refusal to share in both the celebration and the funding of popular religion had been a constant feature of that alienation. Their equal reluctance to allow church property to be used for anything other than Christian purposes had created hostility. Their friendship and other links with the big nosed foreigners, the red haired devils, had marked them out, and when they prospered, as so often they seemed to do, it was easy to assume that they owed their prosperity to such links. The very fact that Christians had as it were chanced upon a new ladder of opportunity for social betterment could hardly avoid arousing envy and suspicion of their motives.

Is it possible that the passage of time and all that has happened in these forty years have removed both the former negative attitudes and allowed at least some space for more positive ones to replace them? Clearly the foreign link in the form once supposed no longer exists. Shared experience culminating in the Cultural Revolution has broken down some walls of suspicion. To the extent that village life has become more secularized, less centred on popular religion and its festivals, other forms of religious faith and activities are less alienating. And the positive virtues which at least some Christians display, in their work, their homes, their family relationships, both merit and obtain official approval and commendation. Does the fact that so much of popular religion is now classified as superstition, and that pragmatic consideration of economic and social necessity rather than *fengshui* determine decisions, mean that Christians are now easily identified with the majority secular opinion rather than a minority religious standpoint? In such an atmosphere do the good qualities which they endeavour to promote find a more ready recognition, especially when they correspond to those which produce model workers, home makers or other good citizens? Whereas the former social service undertaken by Christians, medical or educational, was always suspect as directed towards evangelism, does the state control now exercised mean, paradoxically, that Christians serving as medical staff or teachers can be credited with their faith proving a social benefit, which also brings evangelistic results?

The efforts of many Christians to present their own form of a united front, to be 'post denominational', 'seeking the common ground while reserving differences', has also contributed to this new context. No longer identified with denominational differences which were often more significant for their national associations than theological justification, (English Presbyterians, American Baptists, German Lutherans,) it allows the longing for a single Chinese Church to have space to grow, and to achieve its own form of unity. No longer, at least in theory, regarded as belonging to a foreign religion, but treated the same as adherents of other religions in China, it reduces another form of alienation and also challenges Christians to affirm their Chinese quality.

A change of context at the local level in town and village. A change of context in relationships between Christians. The greatest change of context is surely that of the relationship between Church and State. It can be claimed that it was traditional Christian faith, often preserved in the same forms received from previous generations, which kept the flame burning, but it may equally well be argued that it was the desire of Christian leaders at the time of Liberation both to affirm their commitment to the 'New China' and to negotiate a place for the Church within it which has also been of decisive importance. The place they found was not one which appealed to their former missionary colleagues, brought up in different traditions, but it was very close to the place which religion had normally held within Chinese society, virtually a department of state rather than separate from it. Was it not the assumption that such a relationship was a universal norm which has made it so difficult for Chinese, educated and uneducated alike, not to assume that those who came as missionaries, however much they denied it, were government agents? And on the other hand, was it not also too easily assumed by those outside China that to take such a place was to compromise the faith that Chinese Christians professed? Time has shown that the step which was taken did not eliminate the need for continual vigilance to ensure that the religious freedom promised should be observed. But time has also shown that Christian faith can grow and spread in the conditions, and not, as some would say, in spite of the conditions of the last forty years. To accept the place where religion has traditionally been located in Chinese society is not to deny that Jesus is Lord. It may in fact be an essential step towards becoming rooted in Chinese soil.

Have the changes to be seen within the life of Christians in China finally exorcised those ghosts of opium traders, of gunboats, of unequal treaties and China's humiliation which haunted the Christian community in the past? What skeletons are still in the cupboard? Has the attitude of insensitive cultural superiority displayed by missionaries among others now been forgotten, or forgiven, or accepted as belonging to past history? As Chinese Christians make their increasing contribution to the life and wellbeing of their country, there may be detected growing appreciation of both the Christian motivation as well as the positive qualities of missionary service even when the context of it is deplored. But we should not presume too much. There is still the question, how much have we changed?

~ a pregnant although fuzzy personal meditation by G.H. on the changes in Ch. Xty, esp. in links to State, based on several visits to his area of work 1945-50, Shantou, Guangdong.

10. THE CHRISTIAN CHINESE ENCOUNTER

Adrian Hastings

The history of the relationship between Christianity and China is an exceptionally fascinating one, both in principle and because it includes a number of moments in which some sort of breakthrough seemed possible. There was the early Nestorian mission and its development into a considerable Mongol church in the time of the Mongol emperors, the arrival of Franciscans at Beijing at the end of the thirteenth century and John of Monte Corvino's establishment there as archbishop. John was certainly a remarkable man, but his church, like the Nestorian, was largely a Mongol one and both collapsed when the Mongol dynasty was overthrown by the Ming. Still more promising was the seventeenth century saga beginning with the work of Matteo Ricci. Christianity is inherently a world religion and a missionary one while China is the greatest country in the world. These two great traditions, both central to the history of humanity, inherently challenge one another. It would indeed be surprising if the former had not sought out the latter and if the challenge of China had not drawn some particularly remarkable men. It did. The excitement of the seeming near breakthrough in the seventeenth century especially depends above all upon the intellectual and moral quality of men like Ricci and Adam Schall. It was that quality which the emperors and Chinese cultivated society appreciated. What is striking upon both sides is an absence of rigidity, the space for a good deal of give and take. Each of these moments proved, however, to be a false dawn. Among the missionaries European religious inflexibility prevailed over a temporary Jesuit commitment to adaptation, while the basic commitment of China to Chineseness was never in question. Moreover, it is crucial to place the China Christianity relationship within the context of China's own pluralist religious tradition and the religious ambiguity of what one may call Confucianism. The core of the tradition looks remarkably secular, transcending its village ancestor cult and expressed in an art, a poetry, a philosophy that is clearly distinguishable from Taoism or Buddhism. While both these religions, and even Islam, have entered into the Chinese tradition more deeply than did Christianity, they were far indeed from engrossing its central vision. Missionaries in many centuries sought to convert China to Christianity but the best plausible breakthrough was probably no more than full acceptance within a genuinely Chinese pluralism, as a sort of junior brother to Taoism or Buddhism in relating religiously to the rich diversity of Confucianist humanism.

Fifty years ago another such breakthrough seemed to some about to happen. Despite the often appallingly imperialist and culturally insensitive character of nineteenth and twentieth century Christian mission in China, Catholic and

Protestant, the circumstances of the late 1930s and 1940s provided a brief but sharp glimmer of hope that a truly Chinese Christianity might now really be about to emerge. If the emperor never did become a Christian in the seventeenth century, Chiang Kai Shek did become a Methodist in 1930. The Pope did rescind the condemnation of the Chinese Rites in 1939. Chinese bishops did begin to multiply with the establishment of the Chinese hierarchy in 1946. There was a first Chinese Cardinal. In Vincent Lebbe, the man behind the appointment of the first Chinese bishops, one may find the missionary most sensitive to Chinese culture since the seventeenth century. In works like John Wu's *Beyond East and West* and Dom Pierre Celestin Lou's *Ways of Confucius and of Christ* the long sterility of Chinese Catholicism seemed to be coming to an end.

This was my own moment of entry into the long encounter in the early 1950s in the College of Propaganda Fide in Rome, sharing life with thirty or more Chinese seminarians and priests (people like Gabriel Li, with whom I was ordained in 1955 or, a little later, the very different figure of Francis Hsu, subsequently the first Chinese bishop of Hong Kong). I discovered their admiration for Archbishop Yu Bin and Vincent Lebbe, but also their sense of having been ground down by generations of insensitive missionaries. It was natural, when struggling with the Japanese war and allied with Britain and the United States, that some people should turn to the Christian option with a new enthusiasm. Fighting Nazism, the west had itself stressed its Christian character a little simply. For a moment a more liberal missionary leadership than had previously existed, Chiang Kai-shek's official policies and the wartime stance of the governments of the West could all suggest that Christianity went well with democracy, the triumph of Chinese nationalism and modernisation. That, I think, is how my Chinese friends had wanted to see it but, of course, by 1953 when I went to Rome this latest breakthrough had already proved to be just one more false dawn. The triumph of Communism in 1949 brought a very different reality. Chinese Christianity entered instead into what, to the outsider at least, seemed a long dark tunnel.

The tunnel may well have been extremely necessary to clear away generations of misunderstanding between missionary Europeanism and the Chinese cultural tradition. Instead Marxism now held the stage, an alternative form of western intellectual export, one in reality no less ossified in its Stalinist form but less fettered within China by a reputation for oppression. For Christians inside China the new predicament was both exhilarating and threatening, at first exhilarating in so far as it involved an experience of freedom from western surveillance to create for the first time without missionary involvement a truly Chinese church. From 1957 the threat to the existence of the Chinese Church itself became increasingly clear. Yet in fact Christianity survived even the almost total public suppression of the years of the Cultural Revolution far better than western observers had believed possible.

Forty years later the post-World War II Marxist empire from Berlin to the Pacific suddenly began to crumble, loathed and rejected for the oppression to which it had led. In China alone of major countries the wind of change has failed to blow decisively and communist power remains for the present unchallenged and enigmatic. It is at present simply impossible to predict the shape the post June 1989 Chinese regime will maintain. It may be only a matter of time before a new formally non-communist political era begins here too, but it may also be that the ending of the Cultural Revolution already brought from the beginning of the 1980s a new political era more acceptable to the majority of Chinese, the farmers above all, than most Western observers realise. It could then be that China will continue indefinitely, if alone, as the standard bearer for a Marxism, or at least a socialism, become its specific national orthodoxy: a paradoxical destiny for both China and Marxism, but by no means an impossible one. "Only Socialism can save China" used to be the watchword. Since 1989 the claim has been reversed, whether playfully or significantly: "Only China can save Socialism". It may not be a meaningless, or even a too paradoxical, assertion. There appears much in common between an ethical socialism and China's perennial ideal. There is no reason why China should ape the currently fashionable anti-socialism of the West. On the contrary it could prove the case, and be widely beneficial, that socialism survives in the world primarily in a Chinese form, though doubtless not its present form. If it does so, the reason is likely to be not that a neo-Stalinist tyranny is prolonged indefinitely, but that most non-academic Chinese, including Chinese Christians, are actually more content with the compromise already achieved in the 1980s between socialism and freedom than Western observers recognise.

What is absolutely clear, already since the end of the Cultural Revolution ten years ago, is that Chinese Christianity is not only surviving but growing. In some places undoubtedly growing quite fast and in a variety of forms, with many hundreds of churches reopened or newly built. We know too little of the details and some reports may well be much exaggerated. But it is clear that particularly among Catholics, and in the past the large majority of Chinese Christians were Catholics, there is in the revival a striking measure of restorationism. It is almost exactly the doctrinal and ritual Catholicism of the pre-World War II period which is, on the surface at least, being resurrected: a Catholicism unaffected by Vatican II. This is, of course, hardly surprising and something not too dissimilar is happening in much of Eastern Europe. The history of half a century of world Christianity has simply, more or less inevitably, been passed by. It may even be that the more imaginative aspects of the little Chinese Catholic renaissance of the pre-1949 years have also been forgotten, though it may be in them, in the work of people connected with Vincent Lebbe in particular, that one could most usefully look for guidance in what is now developing. Unfortunately the pressure is in a different direction. Rome's refusal to allow the Chinese church to choose its own bishops and so accept as legitimate the basic form Chinese Catholicism has taken since the 1950s has led to the development of the 'underground church' and a wave of persecutions renewed since 1989. While the Chinese Church has in reality only been practising what is traditional to Catholicism and much desired by other local churches, the consequence has been to tear it apart between the dictates of Rome and those of Beijing. Whether this rather special conflict will long continue we cannot know but while certainly serious, it remains relatively marginal to the relationship between Christianity (including probably even Chinese Catholicism) and the Chinese state.

It would, of course, be quite mistaken to argue that when we have mapped out the rise and decline of Marxism in the intervening years, then one can reasonably return to the rather optimistic Christian conversionist mood of fifty years ago, though that, undoubtedly, is what some missionary commentators are suggesting. Much of that optimism was linked with the world political situation and the ability of Christianity to act as a credible midwife for modernization. All this has now quite faded. At that time Christianity, both in its Catholic and in its Protestant forms, had a great stability to it and a fairly simple confidence shown in the organization of the great missionary societies. Today Western Christianity of that sort is in deep decline. Yet in areas of the southern hemisphere, Africa, Latin America, the Philippines, there is a very different and vibrant popular Christianity emerging. It is with these areas, their hopes and their problems – particularly, for instance, the integration of elements of traditional religion and culture with village Christianity in Africa – that the Chinese churches should now be compared, and it is with them that they may well develop the most fruitful relations.

It is clearly impossible to predict the future of Chinese Christianity. Certainly the optimistic predictions of fifty years ago were fearfully wrong as were the equally pessimistic predictions of thirty years ago. Chinese in the diaspora are often today very susceptible to Christianity but that does not necessarily indicate anything about China itself. South Korea has for years seen the world's most quickly growing Christian Church. In Japan, on the other hand, after a post war spurt, there has been little advance. Even in Hong Kong the movement of Christian conversion has had its limits. Basically all one can say is that the particular obstacles of the 1949-79 era have mostly gone, and if the more theological side of Christian endeavour in this period was to attempt a dialogue with Marxism, it now once more needs instead to pick up the threads of the much older dialogue with the central humanistic tradition of Chinese culture, as also with the diverse forms of popular Chinese religiosity.

Christianity remains marginal to Chinese culture, far more marginal than several other major religions, but it seems of the nature of Chinese culture to hold all religions at arm's length at times and in ways a little more affectionate to one or another, but essentially too profoundly humanistic to be closely united with any. Has the Marxist era changed that and opened the door, perhaps, in a paradoxical and reactionary way to a greater religiosity than tradition would have countenanced? Has the adoption of Marxism made the adoption of other doctrines more tolerable to Chineseness or would its rejection, like that of the Mongol dynasty, lead instead to a narrow reassertion of the specifically Chinese? It is impossible to say. Most Christians in China were almost certainly somewhat content with the relatively unideological and tolerant form of socialism dominant between 1979 and 1989. They probably sought little major change within the political order and may even have been alarmed rather than exhilarated by the events in Tiananmen Square. The last thing many wanted was the sort of opening to the west which could bring with it either a spate of consumerism or a spate of American missionaries. The restoration in 1984 of Ricci's tomb constructed outside Beijing's Fucheng Gate by a Ming emperor in 1611 and smashed by the Red Guards in 1966 seemed symbolically to recognise that some forms of Christianity could belong inside rather than outside the national tradition. So far as the outsider can judge that remains the case.

- not bad, but 4 pp.
- personal musings on Xty in long sweep of history, & in comparison with other places in world

11. WHEN DUSK DISAPPEARED: RELIGION IN A CONTEMPORARY SHORT STORY

Francesca Rhys

Religion as a theme has received scant treatment in recent Chinese writing, other than in the context of the pervasive influence of popular religion. Three short stories appeared in the late 1970s and early 1980s, however, taking religious belief as a central theme[1]. One of these stories, "When Dusk Disappeared" by Li Ping looks at the way the disillusionment and suffering born of the Cultural Revolution led, in the case of some young people, to the development of religious belief. It considers the effects of religious belief on the lives of several people, and religious belief is discussed on an abstract level between them. There is no reference to a religious community. The story was extraordinarily popular among students in the late 1970s, and was handed round in hand-copied versions. It was published in 1981 and severely criticized in the Anti-Spiritual Pollution Campaign in 1983.

Synopsis

A brief synopsis of the story is as follows: a boy, Li, meets a girl, Nanshan, when both are about 17 years old. They then go through traumatic experiences in the Cultural Revolution. Later, Li overhears Nanshan talking to her grandparents, and learns that she has become profoundly influenced by Christianity. Around 1978, Li visits Taishan where he meets a Buddhist monk whilst climbing the mountain. They talk at length together about religious belief, and are subsequently joined in this discussion by Nanshan, as a result of an extraordinary chance meeting, and by a western tourist who is an officer in the armed forces. What ensues could be described as informal Marxist/religious dialogue. The discourse between the four of them is both serious and moving. This contrasts, however, with the story's low literary value. There are absurd coincidences and meetings engineered simply to facilitate the dialogue. The literary form is being used purely for the purpose of conveying ideas.

1. See Zhang Xionghui, "Zhengtuole shizijia de Yesu" ("Jesus Having Cast off His Cross") and Mala Qinfu, "Huofo de gushi" ("The Story of the Living Buddha"), which are discussed in *Ching Feng*, No 79, October 1984, pp. 5-7.
2. Li Ping, "Wanxia xiaoshi de shihou" ("When Dusk Disappeared") *Shiyue*, 1981:1, pp. 77-134. This story is referred to in elsewhere in this volume in Feng and Benton "Chinese Youth, the Crisis of Belief", and Hunter and Rimmington "Train Up a Child: Attitudes towards Religion and Atheism among Chinese Students".

Nanshan, the Seeker

Nanshan describes her own psychological make-up, and how she, "felt wronged, resentful, and a victim of injustice[3]" as a result of the Cultural Revolution, and she goes on to explain how her innate feelings of inferiority were aggravated by having felt wronged:

> "I'll have no way of ever knowing how I came into this world with these feelings of inferiority. Perhaps heaven meant me to feel spiritually lacking, or there again, perhaps it was because I was deprived of my mother's love from an early age. I'll never know how these feelings started. My spirit has been tormented by these feelings of inferiority for as long as I can remember. And when I started to feel wronged, the sensation of inferiority grew even stronger[4]."

Some critics may consider people with innate feelings of inferiority, like Nanshan, to be typical candidates for developing religious belief. However, in the monk's eyes Nanshan is "a fine child" whose "path in life will be among the finest[5]". The authors also invite the reader to be favourably disposed towards religious believers by describing Nanshan's transition from a thoughtful, 'bookish' person, to a religious believer:

> "For it is in considering these things (thoughtful people and what they have created) that one comes to feel that the world is benevolent, and that one's life is full of hope with these people around[6]."

In describing her religious belief, Nanshan at first does so in a fairly orthodox manner, as for example in the 'interrogation' with her grandfather: .

> "I also need to be grateful for an unknown source of strength. It was this which completely transformed me and made me what I am today. I'm exceedingly grateful for this. This source of strength is both great and mysterious. Some say it is a holy will; others that it is an old man full of justice. I prefer to believe in the latter. I believe that he is seated high up above the cosmos, aware of everything taking place on earth, even knowing everything about me. I'm in no doubt that my life and destiny are mercifully undergirded by him. So that, despite my being unable to see him, I am reluctant to leave him. Supposing he really does exist, then when the day comes for me to enter his presence, I will certainly bow low before him, paying a daughter's tribute for myself and for my family which he has graciously given me. My child, are you worshiping Jehovah? That's right, Jehovah. I love him deeply[7]."

3. Ibid., p. 105.
4. Ibid.
5. Ibid., p. 130
6. Ibid., p. 106.
7. Ibid., p. 108.

Nanshan's feeling a victim of injustice as a result of the Cultural Revolution in turn gave rise to negative feelings about the world around her:.

"That was the only time when my attitude towards the world became hostile. Had these feelings persisted, my spirit may have been eaten away by hatred and envy by this time[8]."

From her present perspective of realising the destructiveness of such an attitude, she goes on to describe the healing and beneficial effects of the traditions with which she grew up:

"But that sort of mentality isn't a part of our family tradition; it hasn't featured in the lives of my ancestors. No, I was nurtured by something else. Now I am full of joy; joy brought me by a dignified grandfather, a kindly grandmother, and by good-hearted aunty Zhen. Grandpa, it is your qualities of calm, erudition, thoughtfulness, generosity and optimism which made me go out in search of qualities of goodness and beauty. My young spirit's development was completely changed by the strong admiration I had for quality of character. You're familiar with the story after that. You frequently commended and praised me; that became a great source of encouragement for me. It fostered my childlike feeling for dignity. This dignity has had an invaluable effect on my whole life. It has led me to have a deep conviction that, provided your own behaviour is faultless, you can develop this sort of dignity, and it's the way of getting rid of all the torment resulting from feelings of inferiority and shame. What's more, it was when I at last believed that, in terms of human qualities, I wasn't the slightest inferior to anybody else, that I was finally freed from those deep-rooted feelings of inferiority[9]."

Meeting Li ten years after their initial discussions, she describes the extent to which, in the development of her religious belief, she is also influenced by Chinese tradition:

"On the question of faith, we Chinese have our own traditions to draw on which are even better. Over the last ten or so centuries, all manner of religions have swept over Chinese territory: Indian, Greek, Jewish, Roman, Arabic, even Byzantine. But not one of these has been able to conquer the hearts of this race. The self-confidence which comes of knowing one's destiny, and the accepting attitude towards life and death, both of which are common to the Chinese people, became a part of the fine Confucian traditions. You'd be mistaken if you thought that my spiritual sustenance comes from abroad; my sentiments have always inclined much more towards my own ancestry[10]."

8. Ibid., p. 105.
9. Ibid., p. 105-06.
10. Ibid., p. 126.

Towards the end of the story, we see the extent to which the development of Nanshan's character has helped her develop a balanced attitude to past suffering:

> "History is past and gone; we should remember it forever in our hearts. It's just that it's best not to bring it up again, so as to avoid causing innocent hearts terrible pain[11]."

She holds a similar attitude to the relative nature of human happiness:

> [to Li] "How can you say that in human life love is the most precious happiness, and the only one that counts? It all depends upon what sort of person you are and what things you consider most important in life. What the old monk said was right: "The karma cycle of suffering and happiness is what makes a person's life abundant[12].".

The theme of China's faith traditions is followed up in Nanshan's references to the elements:

> "Had it not been for the Yellow River, there wouldn't have been an ancient Chinese civilization. . . . Rivers have a more direct effect than the sun[13]."

In these comments we can see reference to the importance of the elements in traditional Chinese thought. We can also see a reference to the sun as masculine, and most important in the eyes of the Westerner (the officer); and to the water as feminine. The theme is developed in Li's observation: "Yes it's true, Nanshan and the old monk both have a similar understanding of our motherland's cultural heritage and of the vicissitudes of the culture of our race" as he is struck by the way these religious believers appear to have developed a balanced and deep understanding of their own cultural heritage[14]. But it is noteworthy that, with Nanshan, religious belief is discussed at an abstract, intellectual and individual level. There seems to be no place in this short story for a consideration of the role of religion in communities or as popular belief, or from the point of view of worship.

Li, the Sceptic

Within the pattern of religious/Marxist dialogue, we have in Li the archetypal sceptic. He provides an important vehicle for the atheist's point of view, as for example in his doubting of Nanshan's belief in God: "Is it he who created her,

11. Ibid., p. 131.
12. Ibid., p. 133.
13. Ibid., p. 129.
14. Ibid., p. 127.

or she who created him?[15]". However, in the course of the story, we can see how his perceptions change, and his respect for religious believers increases:

"I don't feel that there is the slightest malice or hypocrisy inherent in Nanshan's heartfelt belief, despite God and Satan having the same meaning in our vocabulary, and despite all the education I've received in the Party fundamentally negating the existence of this notion[16]."

In response to the monk, Li's perception also changes gradually through the following stages (in the all too obvious metaphor of climbing the mountain):

"When I was of an age to be aware of things, the sort of people who propagated superstitions, prostrated themselves and made Buddhism their profession had already disappeared off the scene, and it was only when I had matured and read some philosophy and history, that I came in contact with some obscure Buddhist theories[17]."

Later, Li's interest in the monk begins to grow:

"The old man was getting on in years and would not readily give up the beliefs he had held for many years. He was already passionately devoted to Buddhism, and would certainly maintain and be nurtured by these obsolete doctrines for the rest of his life. This entrenched superstition contradicted his wisdom and intelligence to such an extent[18]."

Li marvels how "he has mastered philosophy, and sees science as important as well, yet it's religion which he sincerely believes in[19]. He goes on to challenge the monk more openly: "I just can't understand why you persist in having religious belief?[20]", but at this juncture, the monk doesn't give his answer in full:

[Monk] "After all, why shouldn't we believe in religion?" [Li] "That's obvious - because it's not reality. Its explanations of the world, its traditions about the past and the future are utterly illusory." The monk was silent[21].

Li appreciates the monk's willingness to put forward apologetics for religious belief. "This faith isn't superstitious, nor is it a veneration of fabricated traditions; no, it's a faith full of reason[22]." In the process of his changing response to the monk, Li is struck by his experience of beauty on the mountain. "I was

15. Ibid., p. 109.
16. Ibid.
17. Ibid., p. 115.
18. Ibid., p. 116.
19. Ibid., p. 116.
20. Ibid., p. 117.
21. Ibid.
22. Ibid., p. 119.

taken aback by the magnificence of the scenery[23]." "Never in my life had I seen a sunset like today's; the sun so immense, so perfectly round, so distinct[24]." The link between natural beauty and spirituality has a long tradition in Chinese literature, and this tradition was also reinforced by the influence of European romanticism. We see how far Li's attitude towards the monk and towards religious belief has changed in the way he refers Nanshan to the monk for guidance: "I've no way of knowing about an after-life. But there is someone who can give you some guidance about another world[25]." Li starts to notice what the three religious believers (Nanshan, the monk, and the western army officer) share in common, across cultural and national boundaries. He is also made very aware of the depth of their faith, and in contrast, the absence of his faith:

> "I looked up at the canopy of heaven which was absolutely empty. I know that up there, there are countless galaxies made up of billions of stars. But there are many people in this world, included in their number are the officer, the old monk, and probably Nanshan too - although she can't acknowledge so much herself - the great majority of humankind, who still believe in an infinite power, the centre of which is very far away from the earth; the distance can only be counted in infinite light years. This being above everything else, exists within that absolutely airless, dry, ice-cold and dark cosmos, without light or heat, and dictates everything. I have never felt aware of the existence of such a world, but that world exists for them[26]."

Li sees very clearly his own limitations as a non-believer in dialogue with religious believers. He does not know enough about religion, and therefore cannot easily participate equally. In this, the authors are perhaps making a veiled criticism of the dogmatic attitude of some atheists in China, who have responsibility for religious believers, but may know little about religion themselves? It is also a plea, generally, for greater knowledge of religion:

> "I found their discussion extremely interesting. However, I found it hard to take part in this obscure discussion. Of course, I could have used my knowledge of natural science to refute the coexistence of religion; I could also have argued from the point of view of the theory of materialism, but I couldn't talk about religion itself; I couldn't discuss its origins, history, its present situation, or its complex and distinctive influence on the whole history of civilization with the same inside knowledge as they had. My knowledge of religion was quite inadequate. It is a topic I will never easily understand, and all I could do was to stand on the side silently, harbouring feelings of admiration and shame[27]."

23. Ibid., p. 120.
24. Ibid., p. 125.
25. Ibid., p. 126.
26. Ibid., p. 127.
27. Ibid., p. 128.

He also observes the source of strength, or force (*liliang*), as well as the hope, which are common to the three of them:

> "Nevertheless, there is an unnamed force which binds them together in their enthusiasm. It allows them to be frank and open with one another and to talk together so congenially. What kind of force is this? Intuitively I was aware how this force is both simple and powerful. This is to say that in their shared search for truth, love of justice, admiration of human civilization, and sense of responsibility for the future of the world, they experience deep down a common humanity. . . . . . . it's a force which can never be overcome. This world seems to become full of hope as a direct result of their existence[28]."

The last observations are Li's most positive on religious believers up to this point. The image of force seems to be that favoured by the author. Perhaps it is that which comes closest to the author's religious understanding?

The Monk, the Religious Believer

If Li embodies the sceptic or atheist, then it is the monk who is his main religious counterpart in the dialogue. The monk enters initially into the dialogue by reasoning philosophically, and by deducing the feasibility of religious belief. In this way, he is showing himself capable of adapting to Li's way of approaching the subject:

> "You could say that philosophy is thinking and science is observing. So that those areas which can't be observed through science can be inferred through philosophical process[29]."

In a splendid speech he picks up and enlarges on the theme of beauty:

> "Young man, you're quite right in saying that humankind wants emotional satisfaction and also wants to enjoy beauty, but that science can't provide either of these. All that science can provide is an understanding of the natural world. But you haven't drawn things to a conclusion. You've said that there's beauty as well as truth. But what you've left out is that, in addition to beauty, there's goodness. Truth, goodness and beauty all have to be sought for, in order for humankind's spiritual life to be fulfilled. The pursuit of truth lies in science; the pursuit of beauty in art; and the pursuit of goodness is what comes through religion. Just now as we walked together, you said to me that religion isn't reality. Well, now I have a question for you: since art needn't be reality, why need religion be reality either? The meaning of art lies not in reality, but in beauty. In the same way, the meaning of religion is not in reality,

28. Ibid.
29. Ibid., p. 116.

but in goodness. The West has Jesus and Allah; the East has the Buddha and the Tao; among the world religions there are numerous and complex branches, well over a hundred. Can all of them be true? Although their doctrines are diverse and contradictory, each one of them is, after all, about counselling humankind, about making the strong kind and the rich benevolent, about bringing comfort in distress, and spiritual sustenance in the face of emptiness. Therefore, if goodness can be spread throughout the world, it is of lesser importance whether or not our Buddha exists. Our forbears said it all long ago: my heart is my Buddha. It's clear that religion takes morality as its touch stone; and is in fact not at all concerned with science. It's the ignorance of those who followed which stirred up endless debate and innumerable troubles. On the basis of their life on earth, they tried to make out a case for denying the existence of the spiritual realm[30]."

In identifying religion with goodness and virtue, the monk can be seen to hold an understanding of religion rooted in day to day reality. In so doing, he is also addressing himself to the problems of a lack of sense of personal destiny and the development of a hostile world outlook which are especially pertinent to young people battered by the Cultural Revolution. The monk concludes the description of his beliefs in addressing himself to the dilemma of young people who have the experience of the Cultural Revolution behind them:

"Everyone can have frustrations and obstacles in life, but as long as one is honest and resolute, kind and intelligent, everything will be all right. Exceptional and refined young people who have no emotional anxieties may not suffer, but neither will they be happy. The spirits of people who are contented in all things can rest in eternal happiness. The karma cycle of suffering and happiness is what makes people's lives abundant[31]."

Conclusion

"When Dusk Disappeared" creates a vehicle for considering the relationship between traumatic experience undergone in the Cultural Revolution, especially by young people, and the development of religious belief. Its tone of enquiry is in keeping with the findings of the survey carried out recently among Chinese students studying in the U.K., which draw attention to the students' openness to questions of religious belief[32]. Religious belief is considered in the story on an abstract, intellectual and individual level. Young people are seen to develop religious belief as a result of a thoughtful (synonymous here with intellectual?) ap-

30. Ibid., p. 119.
31. Ibid., p. 130.
32. Alan Hunter and Don Rimmington, "Train up a Child: Attitudes towards Religion and Atheism among Chinese Students" in this volume.

proach to life; a questioning of the meaning of life, especially as it touches upon personal destiny; and through an appreciation of beauty. A balanced approach to past suffering, coupled with the growth of hope are seen to emerge as a result of developing religious belief, as are an awareness of our common humanity and common struggles. Religious belief is therefore understood not merely as a refuge, but rather as a means of expanding one's world outlook. Chinese tradition is given favourable treatment. Nanshan and the monk are both seen as having a deep understanding of China's cultural heritage: there is an appreciation of the 'feminine', less aggressive qualities of the East; of the powerful effect of self-respect and personal integrity; of the Confucian traditions of acceptance in the face of life and death, and of awareness of one's destiny.

The story is interesting not least because little Marxist/religious dialogue has come out of China up to the present. Over the last few years, however, intellectual circles have shown an increased interest in religion, especially in Christianity. Social scientists are engaging in research into religion which moves beyond the exclusively negative 'opium theory' and recognizes that religion may have a positive contribution to make to society. Despite the current ideological tightening-up, perhaps we can look forward to more dialogue between theists and atheists in China? The author of "When Dusk Disappeared" would seem to hold an appreciation of the power of some *liliang* (strength or force). A post-graduate student at the Jinling Union theological seminary in Nanjing recently used the same expression in discussion. She was describing the strength which the Christian Gospel can provide in realising those ideals which may otherwise be held by Christians and Communists alike.

Confucian Xtians have been here for decades.

Selected bibliography of English language journals,books and periodicals

Periodicals

Bridge

Published bimonthly in Chinese and English editions, edited by Deng Zhaoming. Has provided valuable first-hand reports of Chinese Christian activities since 1982. Available from Christian Study Centre on Chinese Culture and Religion, 6/F, Kiu Kin Mansion, No.566 Nathan Road, Kowloon, Hong Kong.

China News and Church Report

Produced weekly by Chinese Church Research Centre, Box 312, Shatin Central Post Office, New Territories, Hong Kong. Contains short reports and topical information on the Protestant church in particular, but also other religious organisations and social issues. Some of its material is from unofficial sources such as leaked documents which make interesting reading, although their authenticity is hard to determine.

China Study Journal

Published by the China Study Project of the British Council of Churches, 35-41 Lower Marsh, London SE1. Every issue offers a substantial review of Chinese official statements, press reports and other documents concerning religions. Also includes longer interpretative articles and translations. Excellent source of documentation.

The Chinese Theological Review

Published annually by the Foundation for Theological Education in Southeast Asia, Holland, Michigan. Contains English translations of theological writing, poems and other material from official Chinese Church sources, especially the Nanjing Theological Review.

Ching Feng

A quarterly journal available from the same address as *Bridge*. Discusses a wide range of issues related to Christianity and its place in East Asian culture. Several issues have focused on the church in modern China.

Journal of Chinese Religions

An academic journal, produced by the Society for the Study of Chinese Religions. Publishes high-quality studies on Chinese religions. Contact: Department of Religion, Dartmouth College, Hanover, New Hampshire, USA 03755.

Books

Bush, Richard C., *Christianity in Communist China*, New York: Abingdon Press, 1970.

A thorough scholarly account of Protestant and Catholic churches in the first two decades of communist rule. Makes use of a wide range of sources such as church newsletters.

*Chan, Kim-kwong, *Towards a Contextual Ecclesiology: The Catholic Church in China 1979-1983*, Hong Kong: Phototech Systems, 1987.

A detailed account of the Catholic Church as it emerged from decades of severe repression. Contains an analysis of CCP religious policy and a balanced assessment of tensions within the Catholic church.

Chao, Jonathan and Richard van der Houten, *Wise as Serpents, Harmless as Doves: Christians in China Tell Their Story*, Pasadena: William Carey Library, 1988.

Has a useful introduction to Chinese state-church relations by Jonathan Chao, and numerous first hand accounts by Chinese Christians, reflecting the opinions of house churches and village Christianity rather than those of the official urban leadership.

Jones, Francis Price, *The Church in Communist China: A Protestant Appraisal*, New York: Friendship Press, 1962.

Jones was a close observer of the Christian situation in China through the 1950s. His work is necessarily incomplete since information was very limited, but is perhaps the best of the period.

Jones, Francis Price, ed., *Documents of the Three-Self Movement: Source Materials for the Study of the Protestant Church in Communist China*, New York: National Council of the Churches of Christ in the USA, 1963.

A collection of translated material from official sources during the first decade of the Three Self Movement.

MacInnis, Donald E. *Religious Policy and Practice in Communist China: A Documentary History*, London: Hodder and Stoughton, 1967.

MacInnis, Donald E. *Religion in China Today: Policy and Practice*, Maryknoll: Orbis Books, 1989.

Two valuable collections of translated documents, articles and interviews. They generally reflect official Chinese views and there is little analytical comment.

Patterson, George N., *Christianity in Communist China*, Waco and London: Word Books, 1969.

Written during the Cultural Revolution and critical of the communist record. Makes much use of revelations by a senior defector from the Guangdong Religious Affairs Bureau.

*Welch, Holmes, *Buddhism Under Mao*, Cambridge Mass.: Harvard University Press, 1972.

Major study of CCP religious policy and practice, and the only detailed account to date of Buddhism under communist rule.

Whyte, Bob, *Unfinished Encounter: China and Christianity*, London: Collins, 1988.

Excellent overview of the entire history of Christianity in China since the Tang dynasty. Also covers both Catholic and Protestant developments in the Republican and communist decades.

*Wickeri, Phillip, *Seeking the Common Ground: Protestants, the CCP and the United Front*, Maryknoll: Orbis Books, 1989.

The most thorough history of the Three Self movement with excellent documentation and use of original material, although Wickeri's assessment of the movement and of the CCP is far more positive than that of most other observers.

*Books marked with an asterisk contain substantial bibliographies, including references to Chinese language materials. Readers can also refer to:
Chao, Jonathan T'ien-en, *A Bibliography of the History of Christianity in China*, Waltham: China Graduate School of Theology, 1970.

LIST OF CONTRIBUTORS

Gregor Benton. Historian and sociologist of China. Senior Lecturer in the Department of East Asian Studies, University of Leeds. Author of several books.

Chan Kim-Kwong. Author of *Towards a Contextual Ecclesiology*, Hong Kong: Phototech Systems, 1987. Pastor of a church in Hong Kong and lecturer at Hong Kong Baptist College

Feng Chongyi. Professor at Nankai University, Tianjin, specializing in contemporary Chinese culture. Author of several books.

Stephan Feuchtwang. Director of China Research Unit, City University, London. Writer on social issues and popular religion in modern China.

Adrian Hastings. Professor of Theology, University of Leeds. Church historian, essayist and biographer.

George Hood. Author of several works on mission history

Alan Hunter. Principal Researcher on "Christianity in China" Project. Co-editor of *Prayers and Thoughts of Chinese Christians*, London: Mowbray, 1991. Joint Organizer and Editor of the Leeds Conference on Christianity in China

Francesca Rhys. Researcher at China Department, Council of Churches for Britain and Ireland.

Don Rimmington. Head of Department, East Asian Studies, University of Leeds. Director of "Christianity in China" Project and Joint Organizer and Editor of the Leeds Conference on Christianity in China.

Edmond Tang. Director of China Department, Council of Churches for Britain and Ireland and specialist on Catholic Church in People's Republic of China.

Bob Whyte. Author of *Unfinished Encounter: China and Christianity*, London: Collins 1988. First Director of China Study Project, now China Department, Council of Churches for Britain and Ireland.

Carver Yu. Head of Religion and Philosophy in Hong Kong Baptist College, currently Research Fellow at Princeton Center for Theological Inquiry.

KERK EN THEOLOGIE IN CONTEXT (KTC)
CHURCH AND THEOLOGY IN CONTEXT

Eerder verschenen in deze reeks:
Published in this series:

Dr. J.F.L.M. Cornelissen
PATER EN PAPOEA
Ontmoeting van de missionarissen van het Heilig Hart met de cultuur der Papoea's van Nederlands-Zuid-Nieuw-Guinea (1905-1963)
ISBN 90 242 3225 2

Berma Klein Goldewijk, Erik Borgman, Fred van Iersel (red.)
BEVRIJDINGSTHEOLOGIE IN WEST-EUROPA
Teksten van het symposium 'Westeuropese bevrijdingstheologie', gehouden op 12-13 november 1987 aan de Theologische Faculteit te Nijmegen
ISBN 90 242 3195 7

Dr. J.N. Breetvelt
DUALISME EN INTEGRATIE
Een studie van de factoren die een rol spelen bij het hervinden van de indentiteit bij opgeleide Afrikanen
ISBN 90 242 5019 6

Dr. J.A.G. Gerwin van Leeuwen o.f.m.
FULLY INDIAN - AUTHENTICALLY CHRISTIAN
A Study of the first fifteen years of the NBCLC (1967-1982), Bangalore-India, in the light of the theology of its founder, D.S. Amalorpavadass
ISBN 90 242 4906 6
Deze studie maakt deel uit van het VF-project 'Contextualiteit in het missiologisch denken' van de vakgroep Missiologie, Katholieke Universiteit te Nijmegen

Dr. C.A.M. de Jong ss.cc
KOMPAS 1965-1985
Een algemene krant met een katholieke achtergrond binnen het religieus pluralisme van Indonesië
ISBN 90 242 5415 9

Drs. J.P. Heijke
KAMEROENSE BEVRIJDINGSTHEOLOGIE *JEAN MARC ELA*
Theologie van onder de boom
ISBN 90 242 5335 7
Deze studie maakt deel uit van het VF-project 'Contextualiteit in het missio-

logisch denken' van de vakgroep Missiologie, Katholieke Universiteit te Nijmegen

Erik Borgman
SPOREN VAN DE BEVRIJDENDE GOD
Universitaire theologie in aansluiting op Latijnsamerikaanse bevrijdingstheologie, zwarte theologie en feministische theologie
ISBN 90 242 6510 X

Jacques van Nieuwenhove en Berma Klein Goldewijk (eds.)
POPULAR RELIGION, LIBERATION AND CONTEXTUAL THEOLOGY
Papers from a congress (January 3-7, 1990, Nijmegen, The Netherlands)
ISBN 90 242 3499 9

Dr. T.J.A.M. Meerman
GOEWD DOEN DOOR DOOD TE MAKEN
Een analyse van de morele argumentatie in vijf maatschappelijke debatten over euthanasie tussen 1870 en 1940 in Engeland en Duitsland
ISBN 90 242 3479 4

Berma Klein Goldewijk
PRAKTIJK OF PRINCIPE
Basisgemeenschappen en de ecclesiologie van Leonardo Boff
ISBN 90 242 3439 5
Deze studie maakt deel uit van het VF-project 'Contextualiteit in het missiologisch denken' van de vakgroep Missiologie, Katholieke Universiteit te Nijmegen

Oscar A. Ante o.f.m.
CONTEXTUAL EVANGELIZATION IN THE PHILIPPINES: A FILIPINO FRANCISCAN EXPERIENCE
ISBN 90 242 3409 3

Jacques van Nieuwenhove
BRONNEN VAN BEVRIJDING
Varianten in de theologie van Gustavo Gutiérrez
ISBN 90 242 6803 6
Deze studie maakt deel uit van het VF-project 'Contextualiteit in het missiologisch denken' van de vakgroep Missiologie, Katholieke Universiteit te Nijmegen

Huub J.W.M. Boelaars
INDONESIANISASI
Het omvormingsproces van de katholieke kerk in Indonesië tot de Indonesische katholieke kerk
ISBN 90 242 6802 8

Frans F. van der Hoff Boersma
ORGANIZAR LA ESPERANZA
Theologia India Rural
ISBN 90 242 6635 1

Frank Sawyer
THE POOR ARE MANY
Political Ethics in the Social Encyclicals, Christian Democracy, and Liberation Theology in Latin America
ISBN 90 242 7371 4

E. Borgman & A. van Harskamp
TUSSEN OPENHEID EN ISOLEMENT
Het voorbeeld van de katholieke theologie in de negentiende eeuw
ISBN 90 242 6813 3